THE SARATOGA COLLECTION

TEXT BY ADAM FALIK

PHOTOGRAPHY BY MARK GLAVIANO

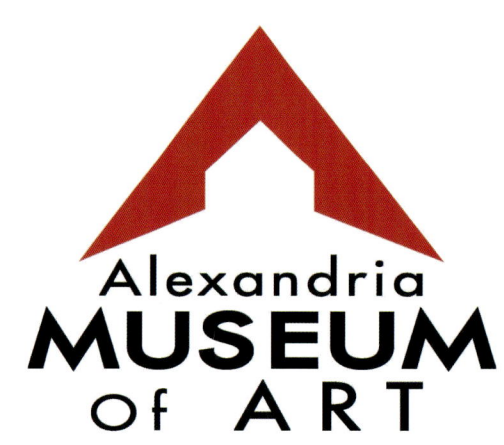

Alexandria
MUSEUM
Of ART

Copyright © 2025 Artvoices Books
Designed by Britt Benoit & Christa Phoebe Gilna
ISBN: 979-8-9912234-1-6
Library of Congress Control Number: 2025941977
Printed in China
Published by Artvoices Books

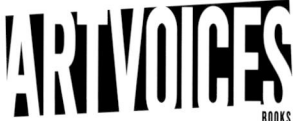

www.artvoicesbooks.com

Acknowledgements

This project could not have been made possible without the help, support, and encouragement of Marcel Wisznia. I wish to express my deepest heartfelt gratitude to a true patron of the arts in New Orleans and a dear friend.

TERRENCE SANDERS-SMITH
Curator, The Saratoga Collection

The book is dedicated to Marcel & Elizabeth Wisznia, my son Lucien & my daughter Maya.

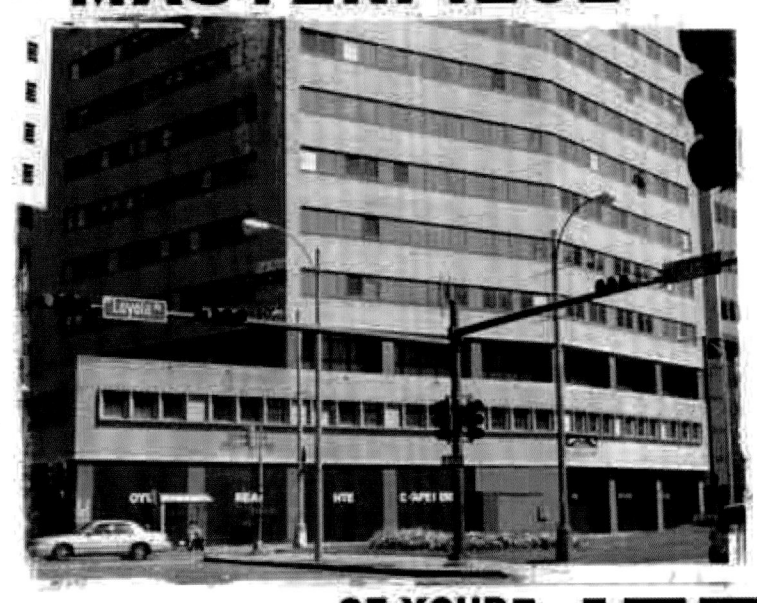

THE "SARATOGA BUILDING" IS ON THE CORNER OF Tulane and Loyola. It is also a bus stop where a majority of African Americans sit and wait for a city bus to take them home. Every time I pass this particular bus stop I feel tremendous sadness and despair. No one ever talks to each other and no one ever smiles. One day I had a vision to paint an anagram on the seven boarded up windows of the Saratoga Building. It was my belief that an anagram would get people talking, that after they deciphered the statement: YOU ARE THE MASTERPIECE OF YOUR LIFE, they would begin to believe the message. I presented Marcel Wisznia, the owner of the Saratoga, with the concept. He approved and I created the piece. When it was completed, I sat across the street and watched the piece come to life. It brought tears to my eyes as I watched people talk with one another, attempting to decipher the anagram and learning to love themselves and keep hope and their respective dreams alive.

On a Sunday afternoon in 2009, Marcel and I were walking toward the Superdome to watch the New Orleans Saints play the New York Giants. On the walk over we passed the Saratoga Building. After the success of the anagram, I pitched Marcel the concept of collecting artwork from 41 emerging and mid-career artists who live and work in New Orleans. I urged him to consider that this was a pinnacle moment for artists in New Orleans and that we would one day be the ones who recognized the potential and value of a coherent and concise collection. The artwork being created in New Orleans post-Katrina is forever changing the artistic landscape of a city that once was viewed as merely representational and traditional.

Marcel loved the idea and asked me to prepare a proposal with a list of artists. For me, this was a way of documenting the burgeoning art scene in New Orleans' St. Claude and Bywater arts districts. The Saratoga Collection features works in every medium, including mixed media, video, representational and figurative painting, photography, installation, and sculpture. This collection of 41 artists not only defines a specific era of this city, but more importantly, it celebrates the artists who made the conscious decision to live and work in New Orleans post-Katrina, when all hinged on uncertainty.

The artists in the Saratoga Collection are relevant and ready to be included in the worldwide dialogue of what constitutes contemporary art. They are each important and should be viewed with the highest regard. We won't have to go to NYC or LA to prove ourselves; the art world is on its way to us! Our mission stays the same: to create work that articulates the human condition, that evokes emotion and creates a catalyst for change.

The Saratoga Collection offers a peek into the world of the new New Orleans contemporary art movement. It serves as an overview of the work being created by artists with a by-any-means-necessary attitude and impeccable work ethic. New Orleans is and always will be a wondrous, turbulent and beautiful city that produces artists and artwork of the highest caliber that embodies compassion, fearlessness, and humanity.

EMERGE
THE SARATOGA COLLECTION

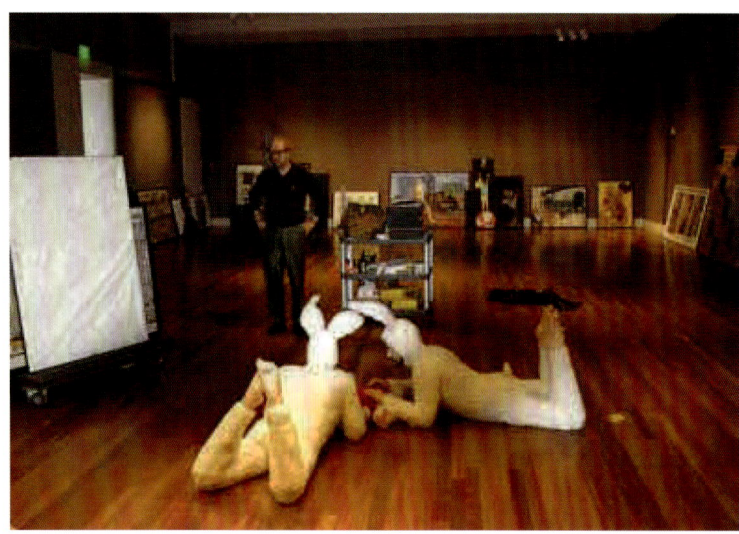

LIKE MANY THINGS IN NEW ORLEANS, THE POST-KATRINA cultural landscape has had many ruptures and unexpected developments. Among the most significant is the emergence of galleries, artist co-ops, and alternative spaces in the Bywater neighborhood along the axis of St. Claude Avenue. These spaces, while often administered by and exhibiting established artists, have nevertheless offered an unprecedented opportunity for emerging artists, a new sense of community, and a climate for critical discussion.

This exhibition, while not systematic or all-inclusive in intent or context, offers a snapshot of the evolution and effervescent nature of contemporary art in post-Katrina New Orleans.

The Saratoga Collection is the result of a partnership between artist/publisher Terrence Sanders and architect/developer Marcel Wisznia, and is the centerpiece for the renovation of a downtown apartment building by the same name. In assembling this collection, Terrence Sanders saw this opportunity "as a way of documenting the burgeoning art scene in New Orleans' St. Claude and Bywater arts districts." But more importantly, this collection of over 40 artists describes a specific area of the city, and celebrates artists who made the conscious decision to live and work in post-Katrina New Orleans at a time when many things were uncertain.

DAVID HOUSTON
Former Director of the Ogden Museum Of Southern Art

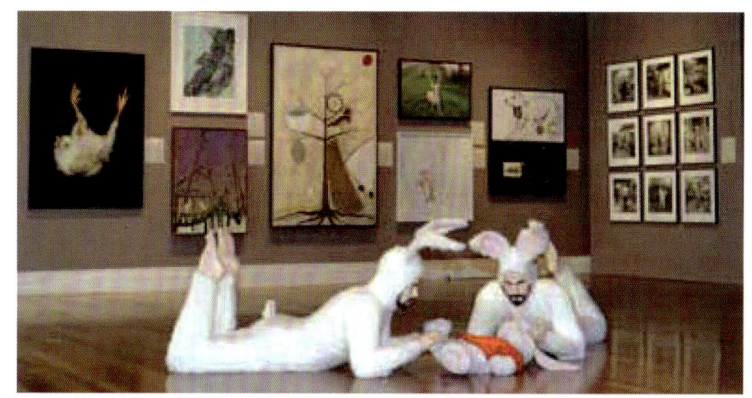

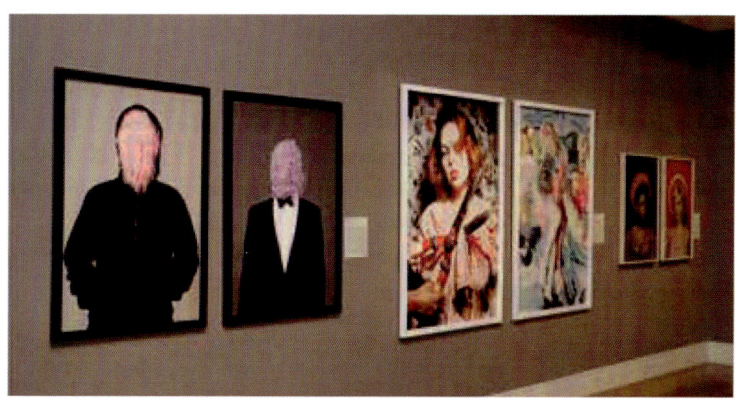

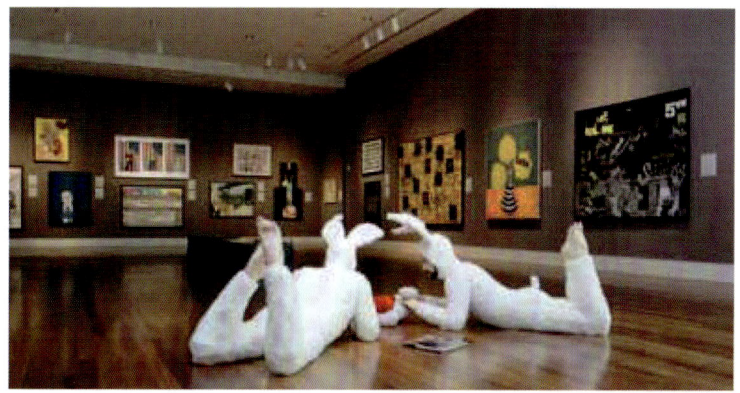

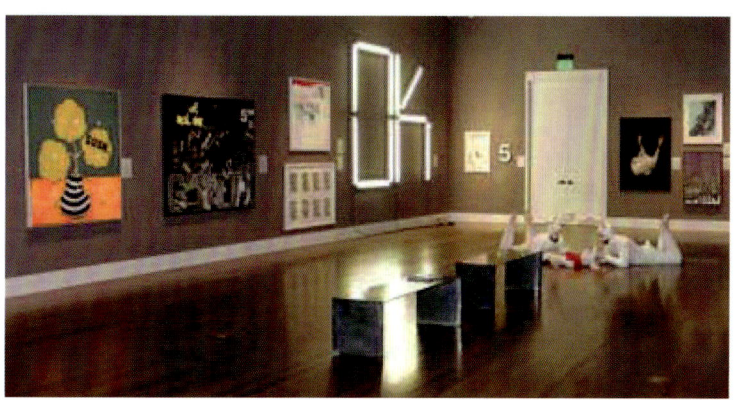

A PERMANENT MARKER

Introducing the SARATOGA COLLECTION

BY ADAM FALIK

THE DANGER IN ADDRESSING AN ENTIRE collection is of diminishing the diversity of the collection into a single discourse. In examining the work itself, as if each piece grew from the walls of the Saratoga Building and not from the earnest studios of earnest artists, there is no single theme, or even consistent thread, to unite these pieces. The collection is dense with paintings, but there are also sculptures, photographs, a video display, and an installation. A census of the work shows a trend unabashedly figurative, but likewise graphic and high concept. These artists continue to explore – as contemporary artists should – the Self, their environment, ongoing interests in race, politics, community, celebrity, childhood, religious and scientific knowledge. Forays into place, memory, and time are not ignored. Living spaces, landscapes, outer-space and inner-consciousnesses are investigated. There are not just ideas here, but statements. Outrages. Pleas. All in the works of forty-one artists.

These works were created by individuals living and working in New Orleans since Hurricane Katrina, which, along with 9/11/01, now serves as one of our national historical signifiers. To utter the phrase "post-Katrina" is an attempt to describe a sensibility, an assessment; not only an era in time, but an era of culture; a flux marked by alteration, change, cultural evolution. Since Katrina there has been an inflooding of visual artists into the city. They have joined the legions of native (and transplanted, pre-Katrina) New Orleans artists to create an artistic renaissance, a realignment of the city's artistic nerve-center. This renaissance's nexus is often sited as the "St. Claude Arts District," where relatively affordable gallery space and art collectives have created a scene, a hipster destination for every second Saturday of the month when the galleries open their doors, serve libations, display the efforts of this new wealth of working artists who deserve – if nothing less than for their passionate commitment – appreciation and critical examination. The Saratoga Collection is the single most expansive collection attempting to encapsulate this post-Katrina artistic environment. The artists represented are not, strictly speaking, St. Claude artists. The photographer Bruce Keyes, for instance, has been shooting iconic New Orleans imagery -Mardi Gras Parades, second line funerals, Jazz Fests and street musicians- for more than three decades. Dan Tague and Srdjan Loncar, while also members of Good Children Gallery (one of St. Claude's signature artist collectives), are represented by Jonathan Ferrara Gallery and Arthur Roger Gallery respectively. Ferrara and Rogers are long-held royals of Julia Street, the once lone-stop for New Orelans' serious art collectors. This power shift away from Julia Street, away from the regional and tourist-bent art of the French Quarter, has given rise to a new artistic map of New Orleans so that to say "St. Claude Arts District" is much the same as saying "post-Katrina"; it is less a place than a movement.

The artists of the Saratoga Collection live and work in the Bywater, the Marigny, Midcity, Broadmoor, and every neighborhood mapping Orleans parish. They proudly show their work where they can. Jim Sohr and Alex Podesta have some of the most arresting public pieces in Uptown and Midcity. Generic Arts Solutions recently exhibited in the New Orleans Museum of Art. Terrence Sanders has curated shows in the French Quarter and the ninth ward; his Jupiter Artproject, which has featured several Saratoga Collection artists, is located in the Marigny-Triangle. The contributors to the Saratoga Collection are what is most easily referred to as emerging and mid-career artists. Amongst them are pre- and post- MFA graduates, while others are self-taught. They are art market warriors, filling vans and carrying their wares to Miami, Pensacola, Houston, and Dallas. While Srdjan Loncar was a featured

Prospect.1 artist, several others from this collection are without formal gallery representation.

Though the group is diverse and multi-disciplinary, a few themes can be applied, sorting the artists into smaller congregations. There are those whose works deal with self-identity (Miriam Waterman, Alex Podesta, Blaine Capone), the urban experience (Colin Meneghini, Rex Dingler, Brad Dupuy), race and social identity (Katrina Andry, Terrence Sanders), political outrage (Rajko Radovanovic), and the whimsically imaginative (Olivia Hill, Rebecca Rebouché, Barbi L'Hoste). Artists such as Anthony Carriere, Generic Arts Solutions, Dan Tague, and Stephen Collins make conceptual games of contemporary art while drawing from the cornucopia of art's historical context. This list is far from definitive. Terrence Sanders and Rex Digler can both easily be considered politically outraged. The photographic surveys of Jonathan Traviesa, Jameson Stokes, Libbie Allen, and Aubrey Edwards are also dealing with identity. This jumble of names can be reshuffled into those working representatively (Hayley Gaberlavage, Aaron Reichert, James Taylor Bonds) versus those graphically inclined (Paige Valente, Chris Jahncke, Stephen Kwok). Robert Tannen is both concerned with the natural order (as are Layla Messkoub, Miranda Lake and Kevin H. Jones), as well as the social order (along with Dave Greber).

Or perhaps I am personally unable to encapsulate these artists after having immersed myself so thoroughly in their works in order to write their individual essays. To my very good fortune, their works still speak to me one-by-one. The privilege of becoming steeped in any artist's process is that the creation becomes unshakably individual, a voice unlost in the wilderness of art's cacophonous terrain.

Inclusion in a collection creates an even playing field. The quality of work demonstrates an awareness of the ever-current dialogue of contemporary art, and an intent to engage it. Most of these artists desire recognition beyond the boarders of their city, are intent in joining the ranks of those operating on the global circuit, showing in biennials, selling in galleries that promote in the pages of glossy magazines.

While more often than not a curator, like an essayist, should be invisible, tucked behind the curtain so as not to come between the audience and the work they've arrived to view, something should be said of this collection's curator, Terrence Sanders. His figurehead in New Orleans derives from methods that dance somewhere between that of a prize fighter and a conniving old Jew from my grandfathers' days: a salesman hustler, kvetching, in-your-face, making things happen with bombast and a threat to burn down the building. He is New Orleans' Don King. A self-proclaimed provocateur, Sanders earns this title by endlessly unsettling the New Orleans art establishment. His primary directive is that a renaissance is indeed taking place, that he is part of it, and that this renaissance should be nailed to the map of now. Sanders is new meat on the flesh, bone and muscle of New Orleans. His ability to launch magazines and galleries and organize this collection, to have the Saratoga Collection exhibited in The Ogden Museum of Southern Art, speaks of his tenacity, as well as New Orleans' ability to continue to adapt and evolve while maintaining its tradition of raucous creativity, even while under the perilous floodgates of Hurricanes and oil spills.

What definitively defines this group is the moment, and the moment has been captured. The collection declares *Right Here, Right Now!* These works of art will serve as a permanent collection for the Saratoga Building, as well as a permanent marker for our new New Orleans.

BEST FOOT FORWARD

BY DAN CAMERON

EMERGE, THE SELECTION OF 41 WORKS BY NEW Orleans artists presented at the Ogden Museum of Southern Art in late 2010, handily qualifies as a landmark exhibition. As the first curatorial effort to lay the groundwork for collecting current work by New Orleans artists, *Emerge* is essentially an overview of the still-nascent Saratoga Collection, assembled by New Orleans artist/publisher Terrence Sanders in collaboration with the architect/ developer Marcel Wisznia. While corporate art collections are nothing new, and even corporate collections of New Orleans art far from rare, the notion of developing a cohesive public collection consisting exclusively of work produced in New Orleans after Katrina is Sanders' own, and its significance as a public acknowledgment of the local art scene's survival is a civically inspired piece of wisdom on his and Wisznia's part. At its very least, *Emerge*'s usefulness as a template for other corporate entities to adapt in years ahead is inestimable.

Let's face facts: until fairly recently, there was simply not much general interest in what New Orleans artists created in their studios. For most of us, even the phrase "New Orleans artist" suggested the kind of choice that was tied more to one's lifestyle than one's vocation. Artists, one supposed, lived in New Orleans in order to be close to the music, the food, and the culture, and also that one can live pretty well in New Orleans on relatively no money. But as far as having an art career here was concerned, there were at least three very good reasons not to: (1) nobody in New Orleans should ever have to work as hard as it would take to further one's career elsewhere; (2) careerism in New Orleans only gets you so far locally; and--most daunting of all--(3) nobody outside New Orleans was paying attention to the city's

art scene. At first the truth hurts, but being systematically excluded from every Whitney Biennial for decades on end provides a city as proud as New Orleans with its own twisted sense of purpose: *if they don't appreciate us, then we must be doing something right.*

Just as they helped demolish an untold number of collective myths about New Orleans and washed away at least as many self-imposed delusions, the 2005 floods after Katrina radically upended the social and cultural identities of New Orleans' visual artists, both within their city and relative to the outside world. After the population began to return and the shock of coming back had subsided, with jerry-rigged living and working conditions soon re-established inside newly revamped communities, New Orleans artists soon found themselves in an unexpectedly empowered situation vis-à-vis the rest of the country. The near-total lack of information about contemporary New Orleans art, which had been established dogma before Katrina, was suddenly, in the media centers of the country, a liability. With national foundations pouring money into the cultural rebuilding of the city, a New Orleans artist was suddenly a prized commodity. Whether they would be prized for their work, or simply for their survival skills, is still a subject of some debate.

Although by now it is mostly taken for granted that St. Claude Avenue has become the epicenter of the New Orleans art scene, the implications of that piece of news are sometimes lost on casual observers. Just as commercial galleries followed the example of the Contemporary Arts Center (CAC) by pioneering Julia Street during the 1980s--in the process becoming standard bearers for gentrification--so today the mostly cooperative galleries that dot St. Claude

Avenue between Franklin Street and the bridge to the Lower Ninth Ward represent the zeitgeist of what it means to be a New Orleans artist at the end of the first decade of the 21st century. One of the first comments most visitors tend to have about the St. Claude neighborhood is that it seems too run-down and shabby to serve as an art center. Well-informed collectors, on the other hand, are usually more than happy to pay a few hundred dollars for artworks that two dozen blocks away would be priced at five or ten times that amount, which is no doubt one of the reasons Sanders was able to convince Wisznia that the moment to take the leap of faith and start his collection is (with only a slight margin for leeway) now.

From a demographic standpoint, the Saratoga Collection is as eclectic a mix as the neighborhood it aspires to represent. For one thing, the overwhelming majority of artists in *Emerge* were neither born nor raised in South Louisiana but instead moved to New Orleans at various times from other parts of the country and the world. While in other small cities that statistic might appear problematic, in New Orleans it is generally understood that most ambitious young artists who are native to the region leave for greener pastures in other parts of the country, and only a small fraction of them return later in life to put down roots. The Saratoga selection is eclectic in other ways, too, especially with regards to style. Like New York's East Village during the 1980s--the place and time in recent art history which the current St. Claude scene most resembles--an unspoken battle of styles is being subtly played out between the post-modernist camp on one hand, who use photography, media, and printing, and a more street-savvy group of (mostly) painters who are more direct in their approach.

Because Sanders lives and works in the precise epicenter of the scene, it is understandable that he would come away with an overview that errs, when it does, on the side of inclusiveness and generosity.

That being said, one dearly hopes that Wisznia's commitment to the St. Claude scene is as long-lasting as Sanders's own investment in the community has been -- not to mention that of the artists. For as impressive as the Saratoga Collection may be in terms of sheer volume and scope, the collection's future depends to a great extent on whether or not its owner can see himself as objectively as all important patrons of avant-garde art, from Peggy Guggenheim to Davis Joannou have seem themselves-- that is, as seekers unafraid to do their learning in public. In this writer's opinion, for instance, about half of the works in *Emerge* should probably be tucked safely in storage, never to see the light of day again. However, if you ask any museum curator in charge of acquisitions, fifty percent is, on the whole, an extremely enviable success rate and is itself testament to the vitality of the scene from which these works have been collected. Then, on the basis of the fifteen or twenty indispensable works remaining, the curatorial/ acquisition process should start all over again, until work by every noteworthy young artist on the St. Claude circuit has been acquired. It might seem like a more tedious process than originally envisioned, but judging on the basis of New Orleans' newfound visibility, the stakes are already quite high, and based solely on the evidence provided by the Ogden exhibition, the Saratoga Collection is already way out ahead of the pack.

Post-Katrina New Orleans
BILL SASSER

*Contributor to **Artvoices**,*
***Raw Vision, Artillery** &*
Salon Magazine

OVER THE PAST TWO YEARS I'VE BEEN privileged to write about a number of the artists represented in the Saratoga Collection for Terrence Sanders' *ArtVoices Magazine*, a publication that, like this collection, documents the vibrant new art scene that sprang from the flood-soaked soil of post-Katrina New Orleans.

As an all-purpose journalist, albeit one with an artistic bent, over the past five years I've written more about house gutting, crime, homelessness, public housing, and an oil spill than about art. Yet perhaps the most interesting and inspiring story I have witnessed was the unfolding of a new artistic energy that took root soon after the debris was cleared. Involving native talents, transplanted prodigies, and young artists who came from across the country, this energy was inspired by the creative possibilities of new beginnings and being a part of the life of a storied, romantic, yet always troubled city.

As the poets say, in destruction lies rebirth, and artists—many represented in the Saratoga Collection—were among the hardiest pioneers after Katrina. Just a month after the hurricane, the city saw its first post-disaster art opening. By the time Prospect.1 opened in the fall of 2008, nearly a dozen new galleries had opened along the newly designated St. Claude Avenue arts corridor. While artists of all ages and from across the city are represented in the Saratoga Collection, a preponderance of its energy comes from young artists plying their craft along St. Claude Avenue, located in the city's Ninth Ward, a section of the city perhaps hardest hit by Katrina. Anyone who was here in the weeks just after the flood couldn't

imagine the transformation this corridor had undergone, with artists and galleries undeniably leading its rebirth.

While journalism may be history's first draft, art is a document that carries the personal visions and realities of a time and a place. Future historians will undoubtedly turn to the artists of this collection to understand the New Orleans of our era.

In the Saratoga Collection, we find tributes to the city that existed before the flood, in works such as Bruce Davenport's marching bands, Colin Meneghini's *Carrollton Junction (Story of Tyrone)*, and Jonathan Traviesa's photography portrait series. Paintings by James Taylor Bonds and Brad Dupuy offer indelible images of the disaster's immediate aftermath. Yet the bulk of the collection reaches beyond the boundaries of Katrina with art that addresses the broader human condition, with artists working figuratively, abstractly, and across mediums. While not explicitly addressing New Orleans or Katrina, these works of imagination nevertheless illustrate the city's astonishingly fertile creative soil, which has nurtured its own creative souls and continues to draw others from around the world.

Every new wave needs its impresarios, its big jolts of irrepressible life which create and sometimes fight on their own terms. With the Saratoga Collection and efforts such as *ArtVoices*, artist-publisher-gallerist-collector Terrence Sanders has undoubtedly played a central role in laying the groundwork for the new generation of New Orleans art that sprang beautifully from the mud of disaster.

NOAH BECKER

*Editor-in-Chief, **Whitehot Magazine***

*Contributor to **Art In America,
Huffington Post** and **Canadian Art***

TRAUMA IS A POWERFUL FRAME. TERRENCE Sanders curated collection for New Orleans' "Saratoga Building" is defined by Hurricane Katrina, much as New Orleans itself, even in its regeneration, is in many ways currently defined by the disaster. In what will perhaps become one of the key pieces of the collection, at least with respect to how it will be experienced by the public at large, Nick Hasslock has been commissioned to create a granite mural documenting names of the 1,830 recorded hurricane victims. This will be mounted onto a wall outside the Saratoga Building. Such a strong anchor can not help but impact our interpretation of every piece encapsulated within; it sustains our focus on the disaster. Trauma cannot and should not be forgotten - nor must it be perpetually relived. It is important to recognize that the Saratoga Collection is not a lifeless monument that looks only backwards to a historical event. While acting as a marker for the reality of what was endured during that time, it is more deeply concerned with how that reality impacts the present and future.

Some works, such as those from Robert Tannen, Tony Nozero, Rajko Radovanovic, and Sanders himself do deal explicitly with trauma. Tannen's *Boulder #5* stretches the immediate context of the collection back almost 40 years with its reference to the devastation of Hurricane Camile. These are more the exception than the rule, though - the collection is notable for expansive thematic territory explored through a variety of media. Pieces by Alex Podesta, David Gerber, and Libbie Allen delve into the psychology of identity; those by Rebecca Rebouche and Hannah Downey explore soft, poignant, and whimsical methods of addressing humanity; artists like Bruce Keyes, Aubrey Edwards, Jameson Stokes, and Jonathan Travesia employ their own unique aesthetics of photographic portraiture to investigate representation and perception of individuals. This is only a small segment of the ideas present. When framed by the explicit context driving this collection, each piece contributes to the creation of a complex perspective on the history and recovery of New Orleans. The Saratoga Collection continues a dialogue that exploded into America's consciousness when we had no choice but to publicly acknowledge deep-running inequalities in access to support. In his essay "Best Foot Forward," Dan Cameron situates New Orleans' currently burgeoning contemporary art scene in relation to a historic "systematic exclusion" from the Whitney Biennial as perhaps a more general statement on disenfranchisement. When resources and support are not available from without, they must come from within. As evidenced by the breadth of this collection, it is empowering to learn how fertile the land in one's own back yard is. The collection is not a plea to be accepted by a New York-centric art world, nor a closed reiteration of a traumatic experience, but a statement of confidence in a local community, artistically and in the broadest socio-cultural terms.

LIBBIE ALLEN KATRINA ANDRY JAMES T BONDS BLAINE CAPONE ANTHONY

HANNAH DOWNEY KEITH DUNCAN BRAD DUPUY ROBIN DURAND AUBREY

NICK HASSLOCK OLIVIA HILL BARBIE L'HOSTE KEVIN JONES CHRIS

COLIN MENEGHINI LAYLA MESSKOUB TONY NOZERO ALEX PODESTA RAJKO

JIM SOHR GENERIC ART SOLUTIONS JAMESON STOKES ROBERT TANNEN

CARRIERE STEPHEN COLLIER BRUCE DAVENPORT JR MICHAEL DINGLER EDWARDS HAYLEY GABERLAVAGE DAVE GREBER GRISSEL GIULIANO JAHNCKE BRUCE KEYES STEPHEN KWOK MIRANDA LAKE SRDJAN LONCAR RADOVANOVIC REBECCA REBOUCHE AARON REICHERT TERRENCE SANDERS JONATHAN TRAVIESA DAN TAGUE PAIGE VALENTE MIRIAM WATERMAN

LIBBIE ALLEN

Waukesha, Wisconsin, 1985

NAN GOLDIN SAID THAT HER WORK DERIVED from the snapshot, that it is the form of photography that most closely stands for love. Similar sentiments and intentions can be said of Libbie Allen's work, that her photographs are an act of love and tribute to the friends who serve as her subjects. Since following the Mississippi south from Wisconsin to arrive in New Orleans in 2008, Allen has explored the post-punk sensibility of New Orleans denizens with frank and intimate portraiture that speaks in themes of femininity and attitude. Her subjects are of a certain age (mostly Allen's own), likening her to Rineke Dijstra, whose explorations of thresholds–children on the brink of adolescence, teens entering adulthood, as well as new mothers–call for a consideration of moments specific not only to place and time but to the absolute of the artist's moment. In the series *Girls,* Allen depicts twenty-something women in the intimacy of their own living spaces, stripped down to slips, bras, and panties. With Allen's head-on approach, though the women are semi-undressed, their attire leaves them neither shy, vulnerable, nor terribly exposed. They possess the empowerment of Suicide Girls, assured affirmation of self-projected confrontation. In the two photographic prints on metallic paper, "Elizabeth with Expression/ Nothingness Tattoos" and "Alesondra with an Excerpt from Her Story, *Pink Passion,* (from the *Halo* series)" Allen sets her subjects before sacred spheres. In Jungian terms, the self is symbolized by the circle; within the circle resides the unified consciousness and unconsciousness of a person. By lending the circle the religious context of a halo, Allen plays with the motif of spiritual exploration while safely securing her subjects in the absolutes of identity.

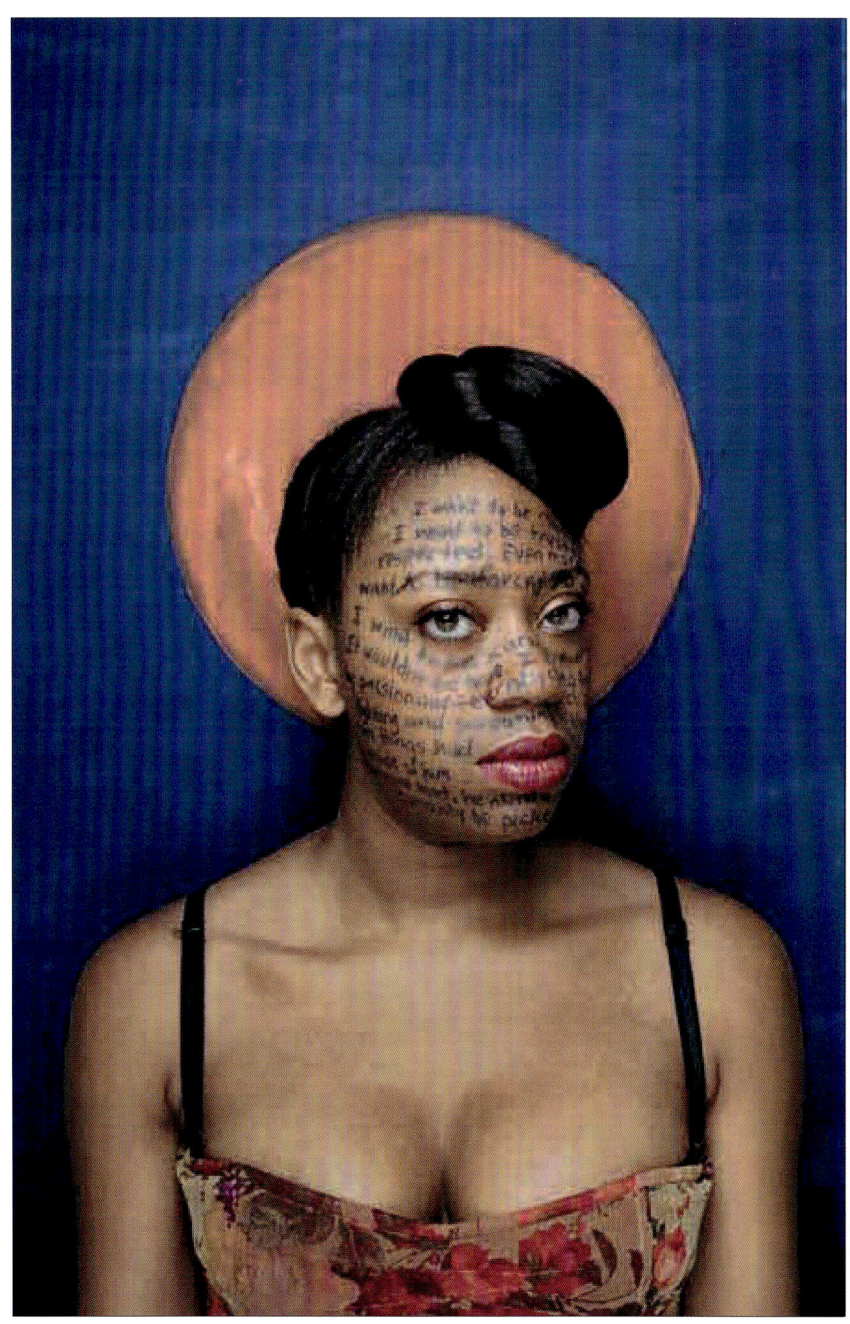

Alesondra with an Excerpt from Her Story, Pink Passion   36" x 24"   photographic print on metallic paper

KATRINA ANDRY

New Orleans, Louisiana, 1981

IN 2010, KATRINA ANDRY RECEIVED HER Master of Fine Arts from Louisiana State University with a concentration in printmaking. Her art combines digital media and color woodcut to create prints of white figures (who, according to Andry, represent Western-recognized figures of authority) in black face striking "generally perceived" stereotypes of black culture. These stereotypes include the pregnant teenager, the welfare collector, the whore, thug, sinner, and misguided teenage dreamer. In her work, *Genetic Inferiority: Darwin's Theory of Evolution and White Superiority,* a white male is put in the pose of a black male sitting on the table portion of an old school desk. He has a banana in hand, is scratching his head, and is about to have his umbilical chord cut, severing him from a picture of Charles Darwin. Separated from science and knowledge, he will be set adrift onto a sea of perception, within the reality of "the other" who creates the institution of the un-evolved, the anti-progressive. Andry's blunt-shaped woodcuts make easy reference to Elizabeth Catlett, the revolutionary social artist who utilized printmaking (amongst her many mediums) to contribute to social change during the height of the Civil Rights Movement. Though our collective social circumstances continue to evolve, we are still engaged in open dialogue with how art serves politically, racially, and as propaganda, or whether art should serve as a social tool at all, whether art is only for art's sake. By engaging in themes of race and identity, Andry attempts to address this question.

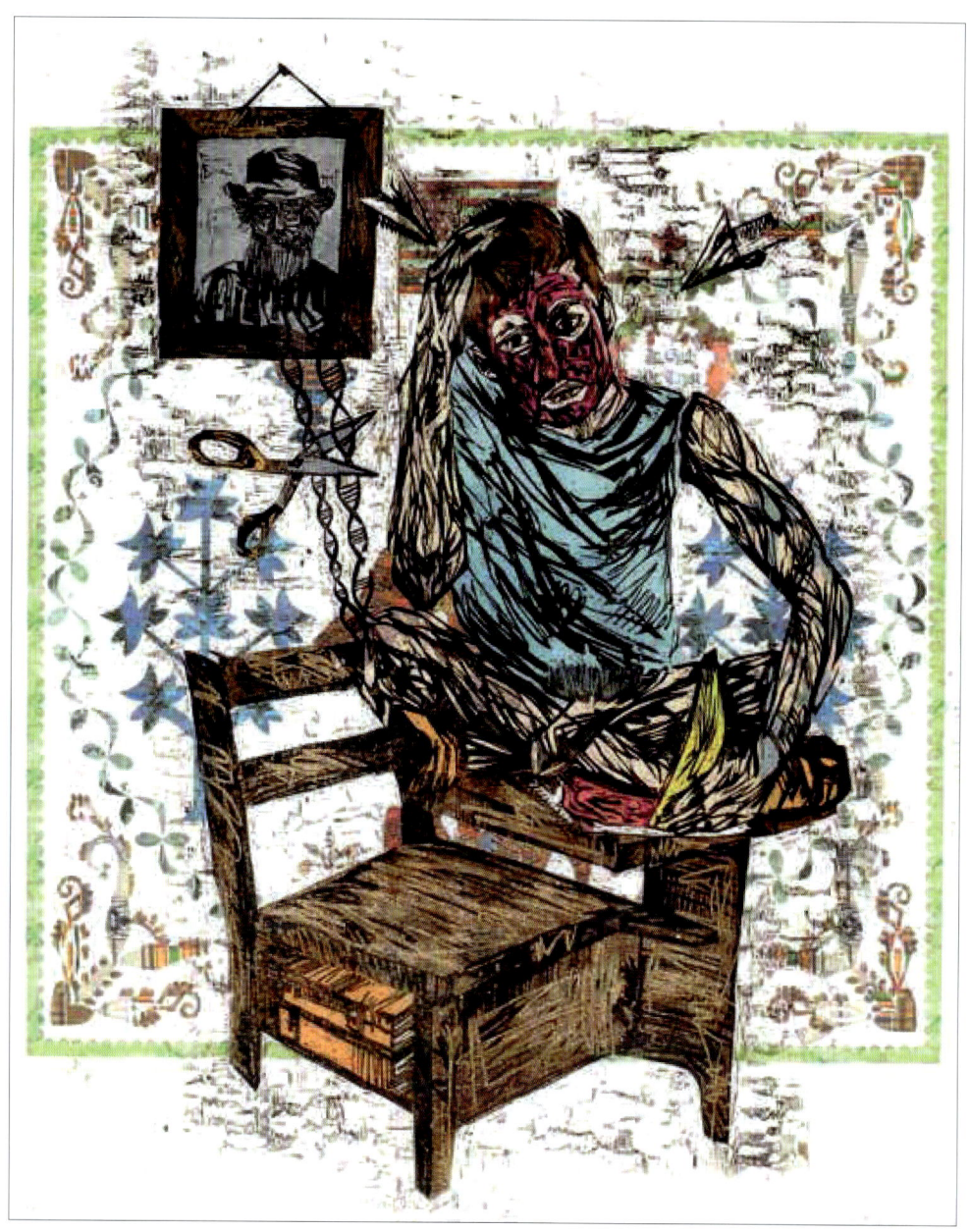

Genetic Inferiority: Darwin's Theory of Evolution and White Superiority

58" x 42"   digital media and color woodcut reduction on paper

JAMES TAYLOR BONDS

Alexandria, Louisiana, 1984

JAMES TAYLOR BONDS DESCRIBES HIS painting, *A Portal Experience: On Forstall New Orleans, LA* as "… a reaction to encountering a piece of destroyed architecture and immediately recalling a similar experience standing on a rural highway in Alabama. Upon seeing a contorted trailer on Forstall Street in the upper section of the Lower Ninth Ward, I remembered encountering a fallen home right outside the town where I grew up … the histories of both locations resonated in synch …The painting thus represents a duality of experience, a portal where one catastrophe informs the other, and the site becomes elevated with the grandeur of these projected realities." Bond is interested in the impact memory plays upon reality. He seeks a Proustian truth where the current landscape summons the pure and unfiltered authenticity of an original experience. This process, though, does not project in a solitary direction. While gazing into his personal past, Bond is also caught in the swirl of the past superimposing itself upon the present. A solo show at Jupiter Art Project entitled "A Foray Into The Fictions Of Fractured Facades" featured a series of all gray-scale paintings. The romanticism of muted grays, which invoke old and faded photographs, spoke of impermanence, solitary journeys, and the doubtful reliability of the process of recollection. Since then, Bonds has exhibited split panels conjoining portraits and landscapes to pattern the multiplicity of memory. Is it the individual who resides in the landscape of memory, or does an actual landscape, like some haunting song, contain the trigger that individual memory is in service to? It is through techniques and strategies of muted tones and psychic displacement that Bonds makes his investigations. "My art is frequently the result of hazy recollections," Bonds says. "A blending of disparate events into one personalized narrative. It is the ingestion of one's surroundings and memories, spit up in the guise of truth."

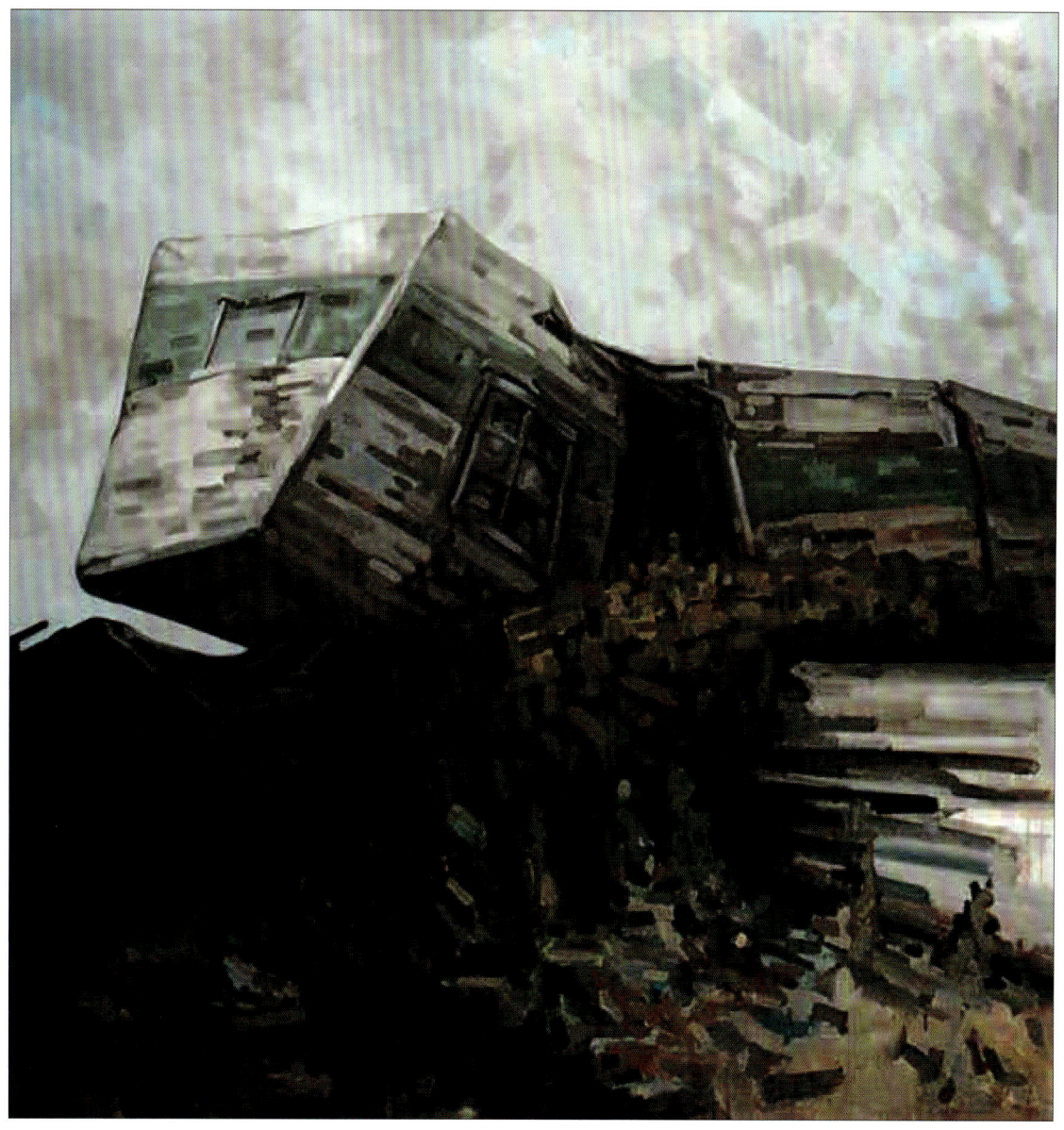

A Portal Experience: On Forstall New Orleans, LA   70" x 68"   acrylic on canvas

BLAINE CAPONE

New Orleans, Louisiana, 1982

IF, AS FREUD SAYS, ALL THE COMPONENTS OF our dreams reflect some aspect of our personality, then some similar decree should be put on Blaine Capone and the many reflections of Self contained in his paintings and drawings. But Capone is an elusive character, a New Orleans native who currently resides on a mountaintop near Asheville, North Carolina; he neither provides artist statements, nor has the type of singular rhythm to his body of work that makes easily-swallowed assessments. What Capone's work lends is a depiction of the post-post modern male psyche, a human persona self-mutilated, fragmented, incomplete, composed of wreckage, shy of its own brother-and-sisterly pieces, and consumed with self-investigations. His sometimes cartoonish, sometimes immaculately rendered (self)portraits address isolation, sexuality, violence, pleasure-seeking, and the need for some sort of human connection. A connection more often than not unmet. As in the work *medicine kid*, Capone often works with multiple canvases that reflect an almost-innate fragmentation in this age of despair. Here a young boy (Capone?) stands atop a beach ball, performing the balancing trick that will earn him the obscene dose of psychopharmacology either needed or induced upon him. The boy is vulnerable, partially naked, and reliant on the provision of an adult hand pictured descending towards the boy's open and eager mouth. In Capone's work there's more than a little Philip Guston who, when he returned from abstract to human representation, painted the hand of God with an exaggeration of human veins and age, and who compiled his figures from parts and pieces. But by fragmenting the individual, putting multiple heads atop a body, setting his figures without discernible background, adrift from a social setting into a coldly isolated and discomfortingly uncertain narrative, Capone places his inquiry far more into the psychic condition than the corporal form.

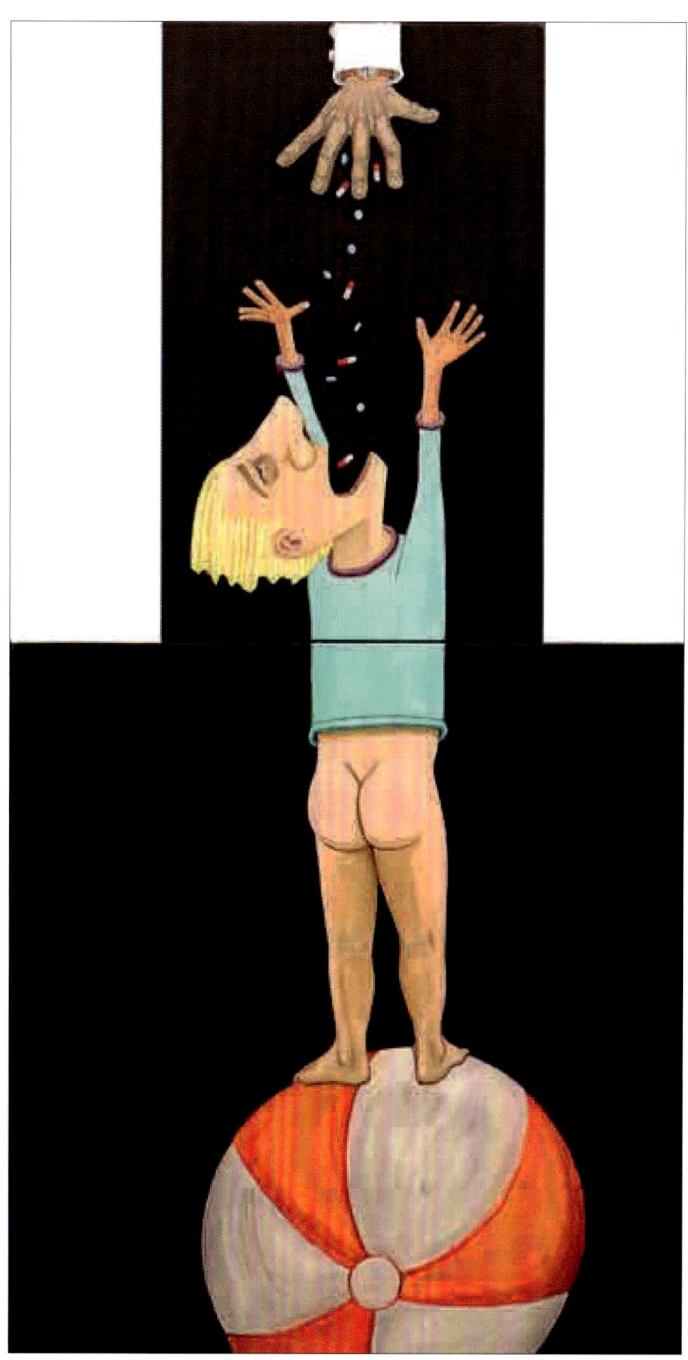

Medicine Kid   60" x 40"   oil on canvas

ANTHONY CARRIERE

Kinder, Louisiana, 1969

MUCH OF ANTHONY CARRIERE'S CHILDHOOD was spent along the Calcasieu River in southwest Louisiana where Cajun French language and culture formed his image of the world. While studying sculpture at LSU (he would ultimately receive an MFA from Tulane), he began to explore performance art, conceptual art, process art, and relational art. By process art Carriere contends that the means justify the end product. Carriere is prolific, his output diary-like. He is in a perpetual dialogue with Self, and his work is the persistent evaluation of the monastic lifestyle of a working artist. A true multimedia artist, Carriere works in sculpture, photography, and painting, his most potent efforts often commingling. His acrylic on canvas painting *GOSH* offers a post-modern pop art still-life of organic life in flat scoop shapes and soothing tones with the juxtaposition of text and the appearance of Photoshop-like symbols, as if permanently alterable. Other works are created on masonite panel painted over many times, tucking away images while Carriere follows each brushstroke, the application of materials such as graphite and copper leaf, to their earned conclusion. Carriere's approach of combining process with imagery solidifies his intent to enhance daily routine into a conceptual act of thoughtful suggestion, lifestyle, and personal philosophy. Art for Carriere is an event set in motion which the artist watches unfold. The final product contains the full extent of its meaning. Yet as Carriere's system incorporates the complete immersion of his life towards transformative fulfillment and his product, the reflection of an ongoing development, so does it require the observation and reaction of an audience, a personal viewer, to serve as an integral component to the consummate process.

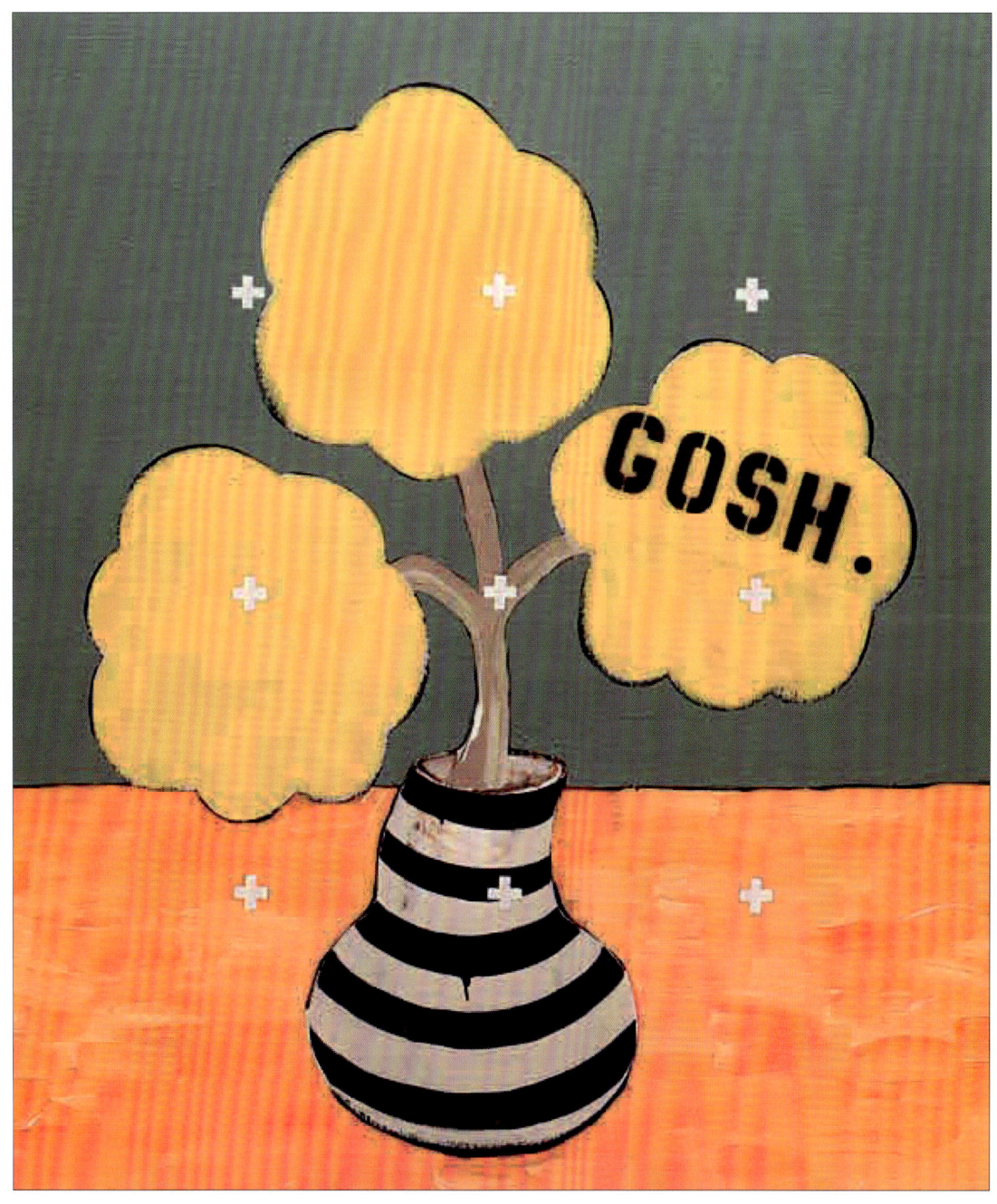

GOSH   60" x 48"   acrylic on canvas

STEPHEN COLLIER

Keesler Air Force Base in Biloxi, Mississippi, 1971

IN A VIDEO WORK OF STEPHEN COLLIER'S called *Five Finger Fillet*, a hand is placed with it's fingers spread on a wooden tabletop while another hand stabs with a knifepoint at the space between each finger, intending not to prick the hand. It is a sailor's game, a rite of passage among men--utterly human, foolish, and inflated with a certain dignity, a certain bravado. Though the knife in Collier's video crosses the hand back and forth only once, it provides insight into Collier's interest in games, rituals, poses, and conceptual stunts. Any material or medium is susceptible to Collier's games. He works in video, sculpture, sound, photography, painting, and performance. Food, picture postcards, 99-cent store items, electronic, and found objects will find place in Collier's work. In "Untitled (Black Hoodie)," a lightjet print of a figure stands naturally, hands tucked in pockets, the jacket zippered to throat, the head semi-protected by the hood. One could expect to see this individual on any street corner were it not disfigured, the face completely covered in Silly String. The same can be said of the stature in "Untitled (Tuxedo)." These figures are urbane and macabre; they might have stumbled out of the surrealist paintings of Giuseppe Arcimboldo or Ljuba, their faces caught somewhere between vegetable matter and cosmic uncertainty. Like the surrealists, Collier's absurdity is serious. While based less on the subconscious than a response to urban environments, the pose of these figures is one of dignity; they stand self-assured, fully prepared to engage. Behavior and identity, as well as the roles and context of daily life are all at play here. The rules of Collier's games/stunts/conceptual stances are uncertain, as if defining them were also a game Collier himself has devised.

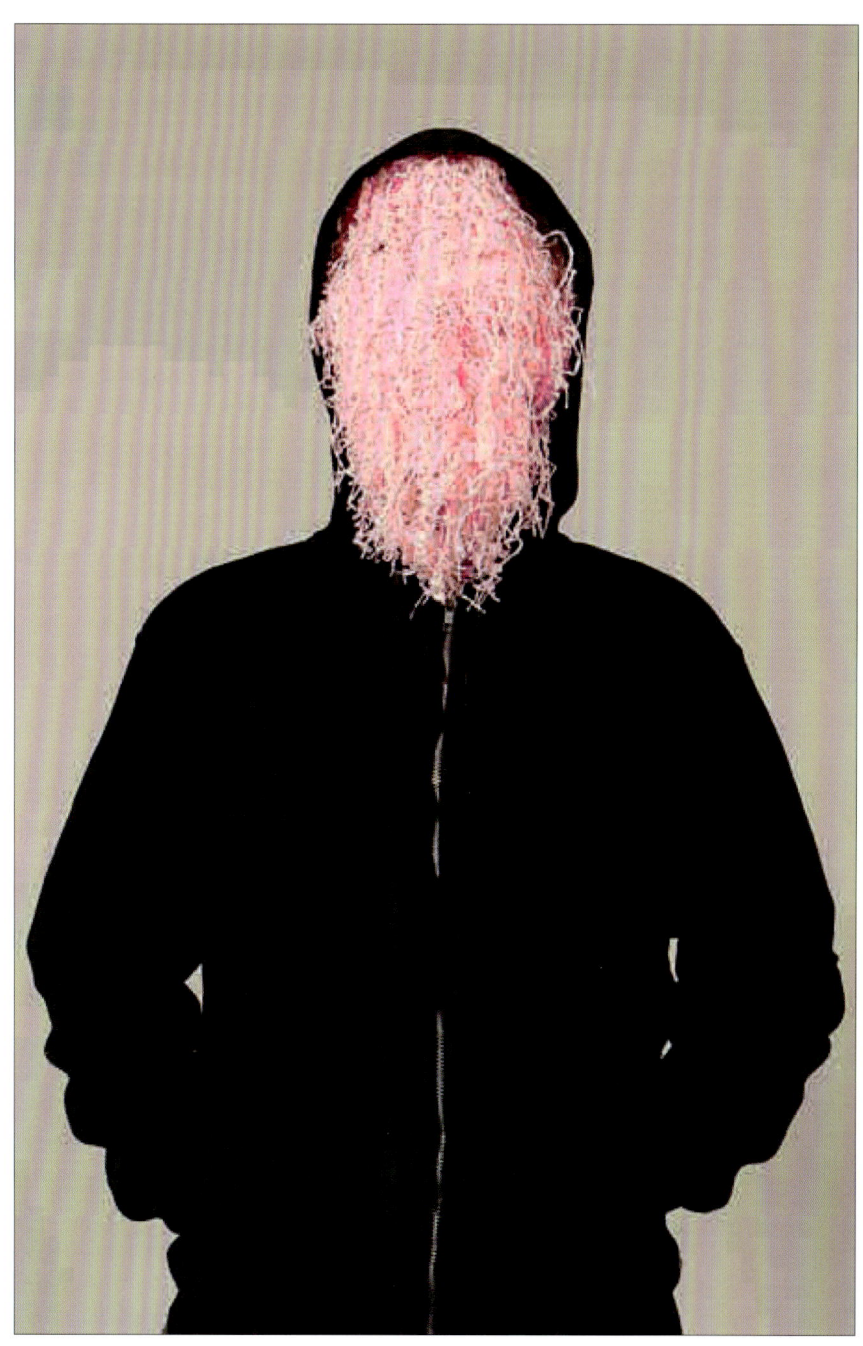

Untitled: (Black Hoodie)   45" x 30"   light jet print

BRUCE DAVENPORT JR.

New Orleans, Louisiana, 1972

SINCE 2006, BRUCE DAVENPORT, JR., HAS created more than 1,000 of his vibrant, meticulously hand-drawn marching band narratives. His process involves drawing the Mardi Gras parades with bands, tractors pulling floats, crowds, and police in the street--the whole scene in immaculate detail. Davenport then makes two photocopies and colors all three. One of the finished products will be donated to the school (if the school is still open; many never did re-open after Hurricane Katrina) of the marching band depicted, one Davenport will hold onto for himself, and the original drawing will be sold. The physical process, which can include up to 3,000 drawn figures, is only one piece of the puzzle. Since these parades have historical context, each of them plucked from the heyday of the great marching band eras, and since Davenport seeks accuracy, he will first talk with the band directors to tap their memories. He'll watch films of the parades. Before ever setting pen to paper he'll know how many percussionists, baton twirlers, how many flag carriers and clarinetists marched that day. Following its completion, the donated artwork is accompanied by an in-school presentation by Davenport, who sees his work not merely as a tribute to this integral facet of New Orleans culture, but as a means to sustain it. Davenport knows that pulling kids off the streets to integrate them into the marching band's rigorous practice and tradition holds diminished value to what it once had. Where there was once street credibility in wearing your band's jacket, and band directors who earned respect by gaining hardcore criminals' participation, the dissemination of the school system in the post-Katrina era has altered the potency of marching band reputation, which Davenport would like to see restored. His drawings literally draw the kids back in. They're impressed by the scale of the work, Davenport's personal dedication, and the integrity of this component of their culture. Rare is a work rooted deeply in the community, to its collective memory, and to its future all at once.

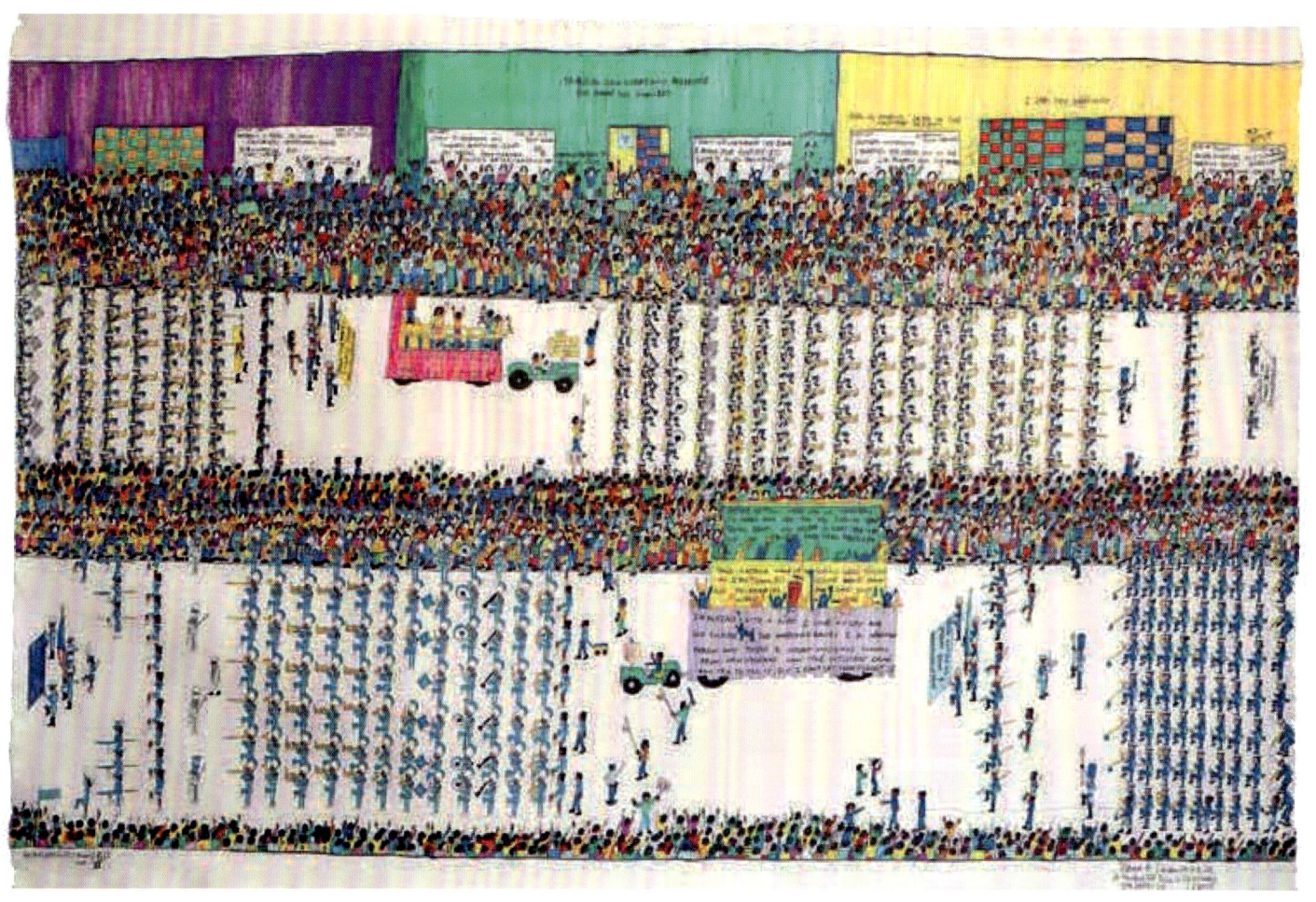

The Game Has Changed   60" x 40"   mixed media on archival stonehenge paper

MICHAEL "REX" DINGLER

New Orleans, Louisiana, 1973

MICHAEL "REX DINGLER, A FORMER U.S. Marine and current ship's captain on the Mississippi River, takes his art guerilla-style to the streets of New Orleans. He is the founder of NoLA Rising, an art collective that attempts to both politicize and beautify the cityscape with custom artwork in the form of paintings, murals, and sculptures. While graffiti speaks up without invitation and manages to question the assumption between art and culture, Dingler's socially conscious work more closely emboldens the spirit of Bansky, the graffiti provocateur who has also made a mark on New Orleans with unbidden street pictorial epigrams. While Dingler has been brought up on charges including 1,100 counts of illegally posting on telephone poles, his belief (which he lectures on at Tulane University) is that street art can be a legitimate cultural basis for urban rejuvenation. His *SOMEWHERE IN THE CITY, THIS BLOOD IS REAL* captures the essence of his street campaigns brought to canvas. The same block-letter stenciled text message with splattering of red paint has also adorned New Orleans sidewalks and buildings. Dingler's work is a form of activism that astutely addresses the city's cultural and civic climate. He is interested both in the man-on-the-street and the streets itself, its cityscape, architecture, and geography, which Dingler also explores with architecturally-aligned abstracts and panoramic studies of city skylines. There is a school of thought bordering on mysticism that divines a relationship between the shape of buildings and the mental and spiritual health of those who reside within them. Dingler likewise seeks the balance between a city's denizens and their capacity to accept, and interact, with art. In addition to street and studio efforts, Dingler works to promote art education and therapy programs for those who suffer from post-traumatic stress disorder issues.

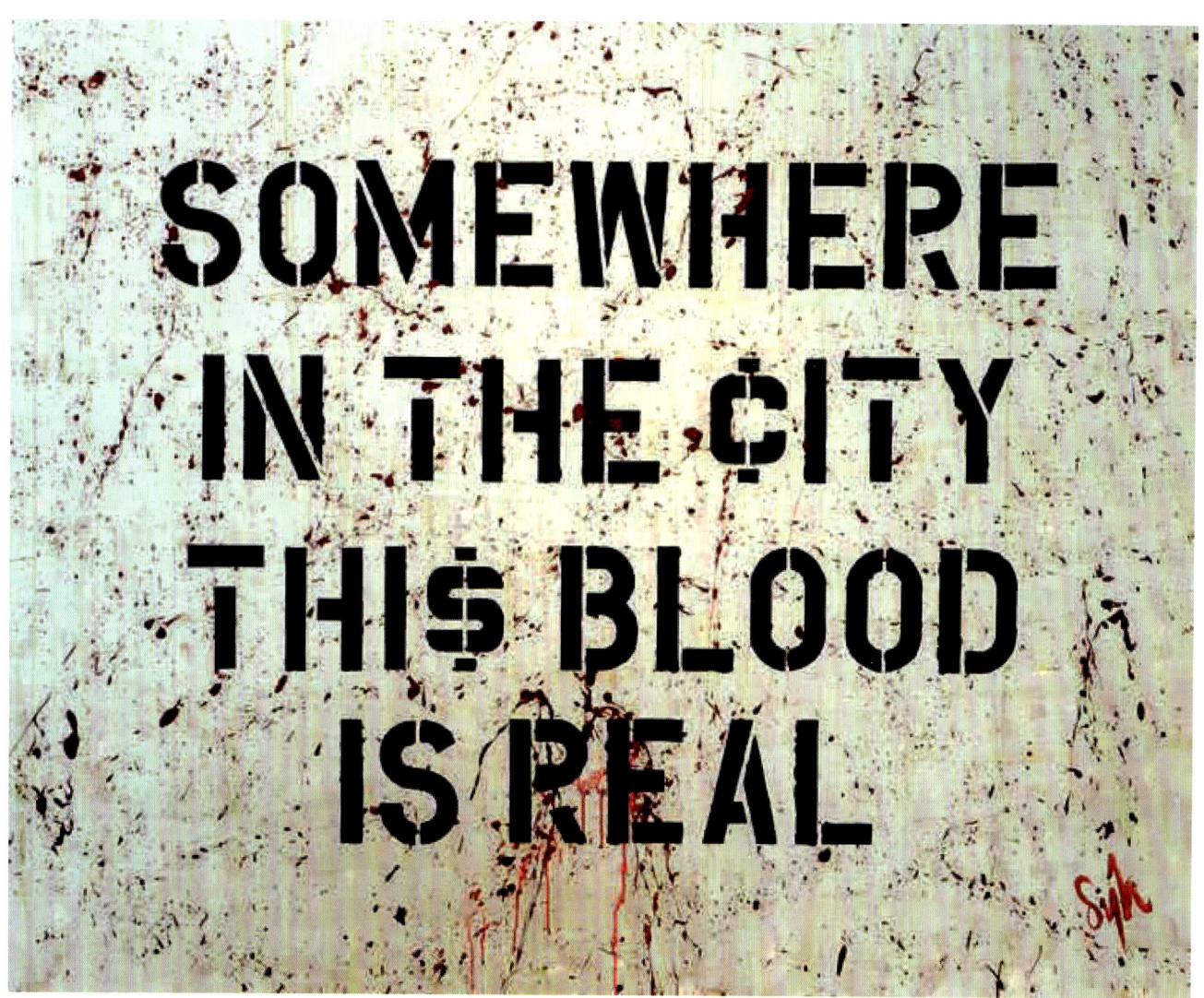

Somewhere In The City, This Blood Is Real   40" x 60"   acrylic on canvas

HANNAH DOWNEY

Houston, Texas, 1989

THERE IS A GENTLE SENTIMENTALITY TO Hannah Downey's work. Downey is nostalgic for what constitutes our animal nature, but an animal nature that nurtures, that is somehow bonded to the best of our humanity. Like a prehistoric mosquito preserved in amber, Downey's paintings attempt to capture human essence at an evolutionary turning point between primal logic and civilized reason. But which side are we looking at? And is it the animal or human nature that best attends to the development of our civilization? The gorilla in Downey's painting, *Exhale* is tame. It embraces its own child as well as the human mother holding her infant. The animal and human find placid symbiosis in the embrace of motherhood. Motherhood is one of Downey's essential themes. Her viewer floats in primal waters, in the safety of wombs and a mother's hands. Her paints seem as if mixed with oil, gesso, mother's milk, and bodily fluids. Backgrounds swirl and drip as if a penumbra between firmament and primordial ooze. They are a wash of white and gray with only a suggestion of blues and peaches. The birth of stronger colors is reserved for the figures that hatch and huddle, creating niche for themselves in the great expanse of space. Downey also creates ceramic, porcelain, and cast-aluminum sculptures of human/animal hybrids. She makes homes and wombs of hands and sets villages atop elephant's backs. Her intent is to explore the mortal and tender vulnerability of human nature more often dismissed by the harsh reckoning of contemporary art.

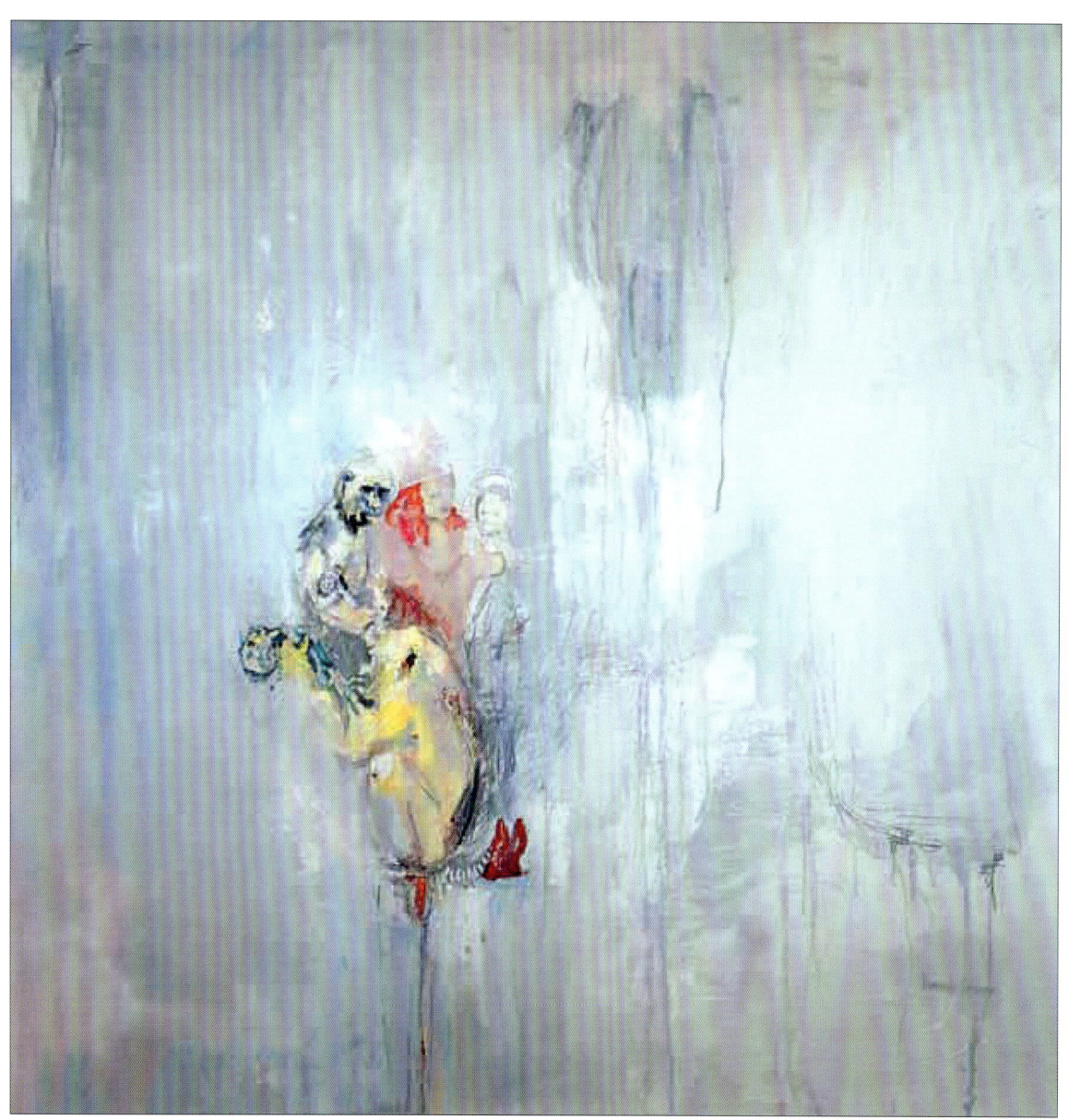

Exhale   36" x 36"   oil on canvas

KEITH DUNCAN

New Orleans, Louisiana, 1964

PAINTING FOR KEITH DUNCAN IS A MEANS OF storytelling, and in that process his narrative delves into the harsh realities of social commentary, his own childhood, politics, and the frustrations and satisfaction of artistic endeavors. In an effort to do so clearly, his canvases serve as narratives in which objects become symbols and keys into the autobiography of self-analysis and discovery. Duncan's iconographic images of blacks in the American south echoes the works of Jacob Lawrence and Romero Bearden, yet his fragmentation and multiplicities also salute the methodology of artists such as David Salle. Duncan's painting, *Upon Return*, depicts an elderly couple standing reflectively before their cinderblock-supported home. In their hands they each possess a crutch: he a cane and she a bible. Perhaps these artifacts provide solace against the oppression of Empire looming above them in the shape of a municipal water tower and against the pages of Time, which are escaping them. Their dancing days long behind them, mere apparitions now, they can only expect their bodies to shrink while the menace which pursues them grows larger. Yet we can also expect them to endure, to remain standing as long as they still possess breath. Behind the couple is a collage pattern which serves as both the painting's and the couple's background. Amongst bucolic scenes of white colonial America are couples on park benches, family picnics, and rendezvous around trickling fountains. Yet these idylls never belonged to this couple, never had a chance of being theirs; and if these settings of pleasantry and pageantry had ever been promised, it was not one fulfilled. While making bold statements both personal and universal, Duncan taps his own subconscious in the effort to transform autobiography to iconography.

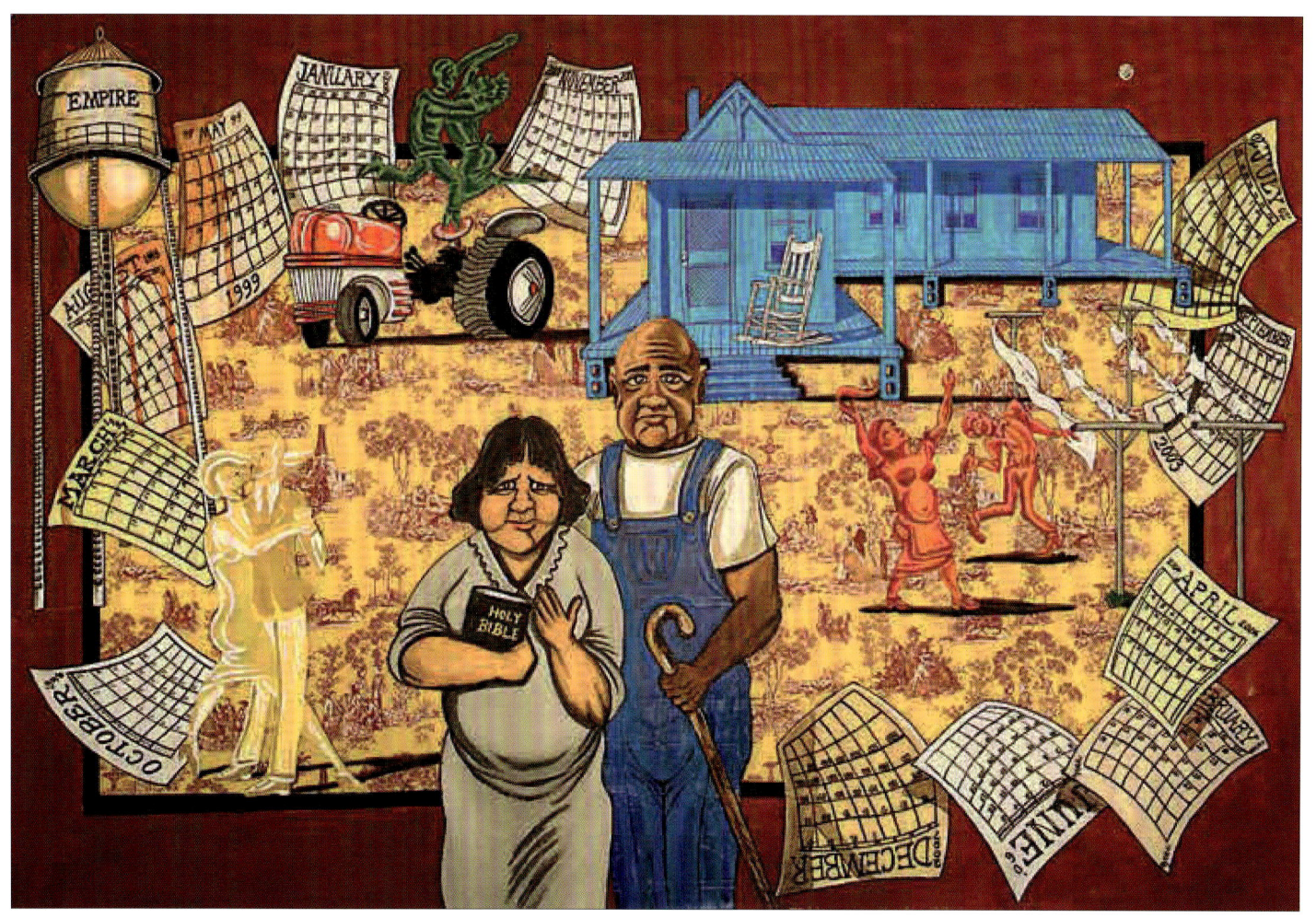

Upon Return   72" x 108"   acrylic on quilt

BRAD DUPUY

New Orleans, Louisiana, 20th century

BRAD DUPUY IS INTERESTED IN HOUSES and homes and the distinction between the two. His acrylic paintings provide the sensual pleasure of strolling through a residential neighborhood wearing a pair of X-ray glasses. We are not merely peeping through windows, though; a fragmentation is occurring. Dupuy's depicted existence has shattered into shards of human emotions, desires, and identities. Using techniques more easily associated with film and Photoshop, such as super-imposition and montage, digital layering and color fragmentation, the Self is often elusive; figures are blurred or disfigured by a host of household utensils and furnishings. The effect borders on a decorative panorama somewhere between Russian constructivists such as El Lissitzky and Frank Stella's geometric mosaics. But Dupuy's terrain is human, not decorative. It is the urban residential setting that is the center of his observation. Dupuy fills his frames with layers of city street maps and fences; the inventions are demarcations, boundaries; they address sociological and psychological tendencies. In *Blue Neighborhood (Open Question)*, the contemporary male is sealed inside a plastic notebook folder like a specimen in a jar. His home environment is destroyed (echoing hurricane Katrina, as well as other natural and man-made disasters which disturb the tranquility of our living spaces), yet the objects which the Self clings to, here a favorite living room chair and a sandwich, persevere. The figure, slotted away, is secure in a world made safe by the designs of society. His home is razed but the lines of his city continue to be mapped out. There's lunch to enjoy, as well as the distractions of entertainment, as depicted by the sort of lame but present neon window display. Humanity is persistent.

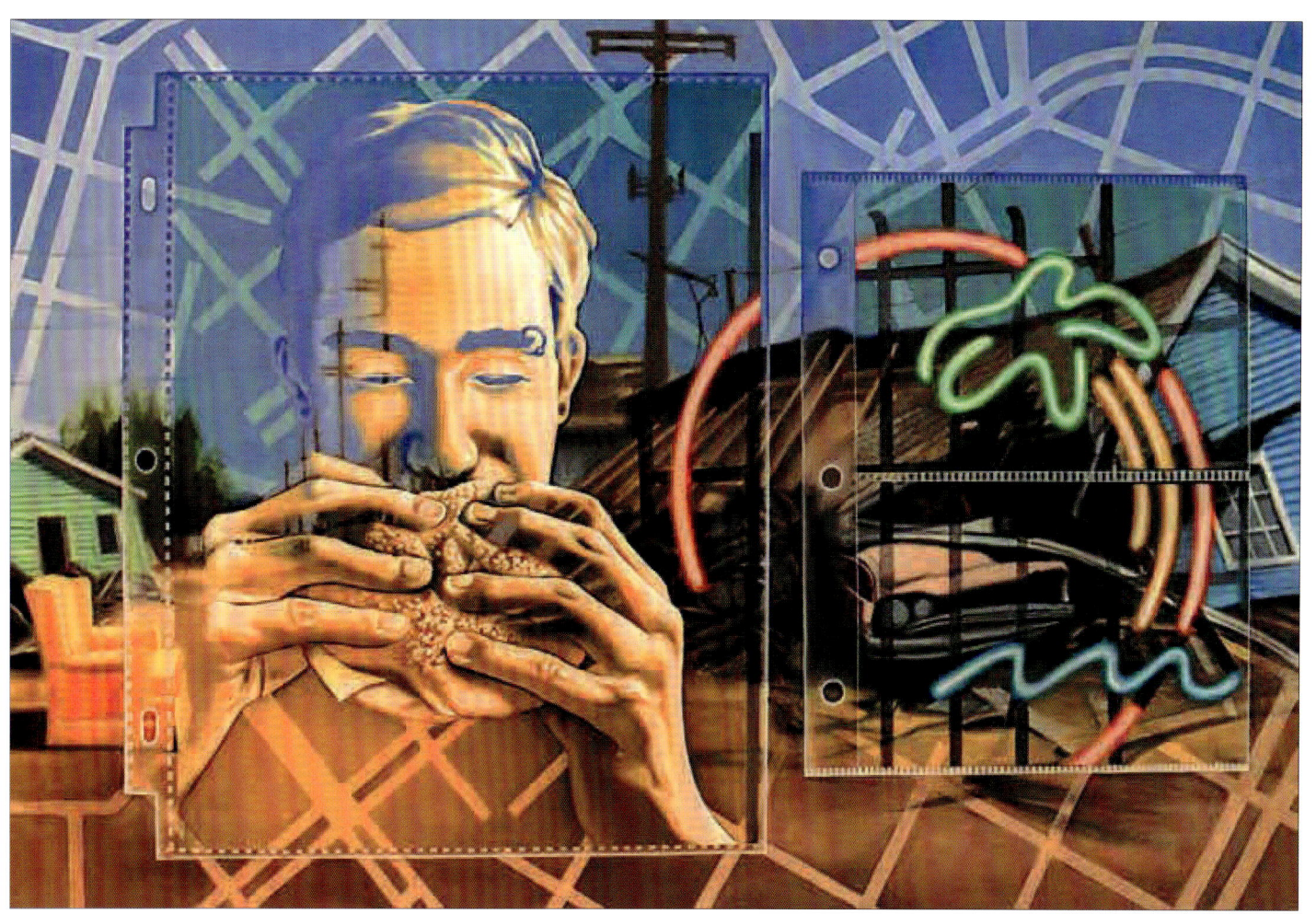

Blue Neighborhood (Open Question)   42" x 72"   acrylic on canvas

ROBIN DURAND

Hawaii, 1968

ROBIN DURAND IS THE SON AND GRANDSON of painters and learned to paint from his father while growing up in Hawaii. He became seriously interested in painting when introduced to specialized color principles by George T. Thurmond and, later, Sammy Britt, Gerald Deloach, and others. He gained a BFA from Delta State University in 1997 and an MFA from Louisiana State University in 2000. He also studied Traditional Chinese painting at the Xian Institute of Art, China. Durand has been painting landscapes for twenty years. A recent show at Solid Air gallery featured New Orleans street scenes in the softest pastel color pallet, the pink and orange hues of gentle sunrises and sunsets. His work *Removes Dirt and Stains* is from his *Mondo Anachrony* series in which Durand referenced and appropriated Old Master themes with twenty-first century concerns. The canvas "smashes together" the logo of Tide laundry detergent with Leonardo da Vinci's *Deluge*, one of da Vinci's unrealized masterpieces, which exists only in sketches. Superimposed are Fema trailers, making reference to Hurricane Katrina. The extreme subtlety of Da Vinci's aesthetic against the in-your-face claims of commercial advertising clash cataclysmically, enhancing Da Vinci's apocalyptic horror with post-modern consumerism commentary. Durand sees himself in great conversation with art history. His interest in landscape lies in its mutable nature and ability to be broken down into shapes and colors. He works to circumvent the habits of memory and assumption by reissuing a landscape's believability in the shape of a new vision.

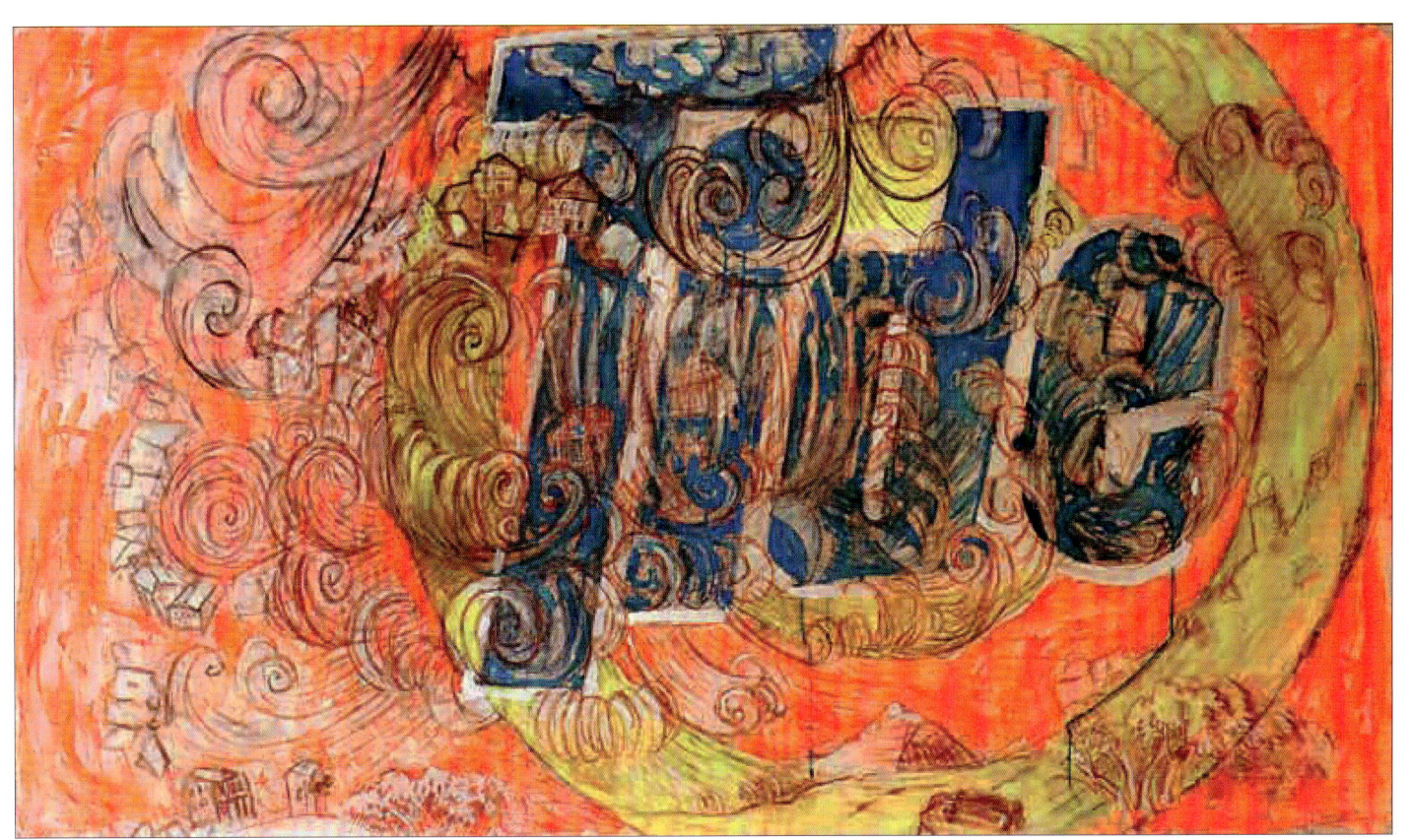

Removes Dirt and Stains   48" x 108"   oil and acrylic on canvas

AUBREY EDWARDS

Loma Linda, California, 1979

BOTH AUBREY EDWARDS' "JEN" AND "MISS Pussycat" recall the neon gloss of the 1990s hyper-overindulgent images of *Rolling Stone* magazine photographer David Lachapelle, as well as the frenetic energy of MTV (back when it played music videos). Portraits of supercharged personalities collide with readymade props shining like diner chrome. Photography and music have savored a particular bond since the 1950s, when the pin-up celebrity of musicians became indistinguishable from a musician's product: their music. Edwards continues the tradition of narrated scenario photography, carefully staged portraits that make characters of character. Like Annie Leibovitz and Mark Seliger, Edwards uses mise-en-scène to draw out a subject's essence, while at the same time lending enough narrative power to determine a force of personality outside the realms of traditional portraiture. Edwards applies a vertical format versus the traditional horizontal to landscape and still life photography. In her *Chippewa Falls* series, a selection of images shot while staying on the Lac Courte Oreilles Indian Reservation in Northern Wisconsin, Edwards confines water, landscape and trees into the vertical, assigning personality to terrain and juxtaposing them side-by-side with local residents. Edwards' approach, combined with her interest in music, gained application and national attention in the *Where They At* project, which chronicled the origins and scene of the New Orleans bounce music phenomenon. The project, in words (a collaboration with journalist Alison Fensterstock) and pictures, was exhibited in the Ogden Museum of Southern Art. Photographing the DJs, producers, rappers, record store owners, promoters and journalists of the bounce scene, Edwards' ability to excavate personality grants clear testament to the individuals who comprise a decades-long community and culturally defining movement.

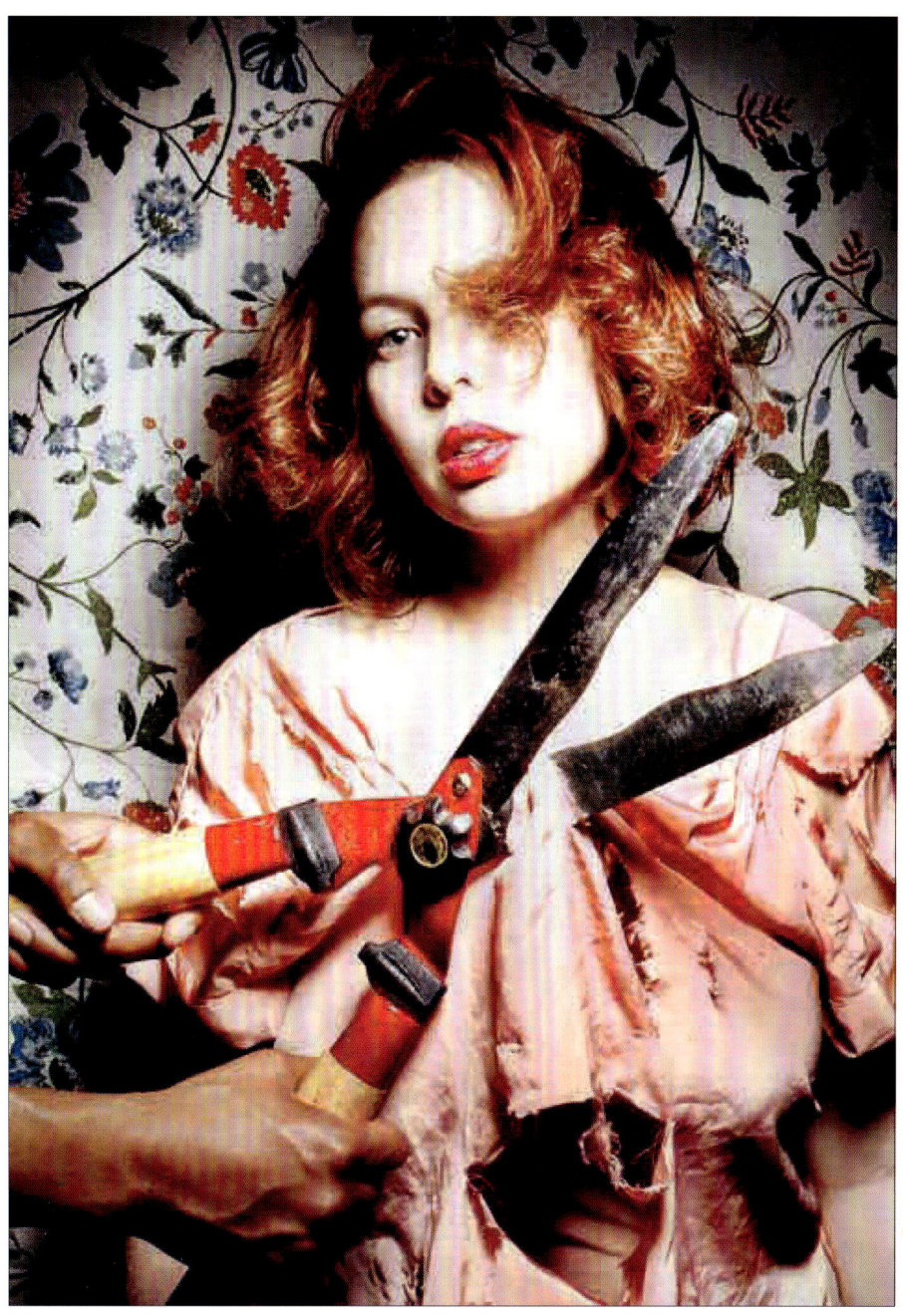

Jen   60" x 40"   digital print

HAYLEY GABERLAVAGE

Opelika, Alabama, 1978

WITH AN INTEREST IN FASHION, INTERIOR design and furniture, Hayley Gaberlavage contemporizes the out-dated with a sentiment for bygone attitudes and appearances. Her acrylic on paper, canvas and panel paintings shimmy in two directions: towards the decorative, where Gaberlavage explores a long-time infatuation with Danish design, and in an Alex Katz-like sociological portraiture where innocence is equally dispersed amongst irreverent youth and the Americana working-class of Gaberlavage's Alabama roots. Her pallet is distinct, a preference for turquoise blues, hunter greens and olives, muted tones and an often thin or even unfinished background surface. This technique of background evaporating into swarthy brushstrokes allows Time into the work, the acknowledgment of memory, which is imperfect, always unfinished, and congruous to the retro aesthetic and mood. Notable is when Gaberlavage simultaneously pursues fashion and painting, such as in *Red Dress*, which features a figure in a huge, swirling, near-impossibly designed dress that recall the Japanese flourishes of Issey Miyake and Kenzo. Gaberlavage's women sustain cigarettes and cocktails late into the night; they wear party-dresses and gather in rooms of 1970's décor. They are poised, stained and sainted like Elizabeth Peyton's permanently androgynous youths. Gaberlavage manages to carry the mystery of youth into older subjects. There is something disturbingly innocuous in the male subject of *The Devil Made Me Do It*. He stands with a blackened eye and a head-cocked smirk in a New Orleans mug shot. He is one of those always-reported-as "good quiet neighbors" that tend to follow certain atrocity. But should his unreadable appearance indict him? Gaberlavage, to her merit, gives us little to go on. It is mood and temperament the viewer is left with. Gaberlavage works fast, is prolific and unafraid to shift directions while still maintaining certain disciplines. She has recently forayed into Rothko-like abstracts, exploring moods with a few lines of foreground and wide planes of undulating-color space. It is the sort of departure intrepid artists make.

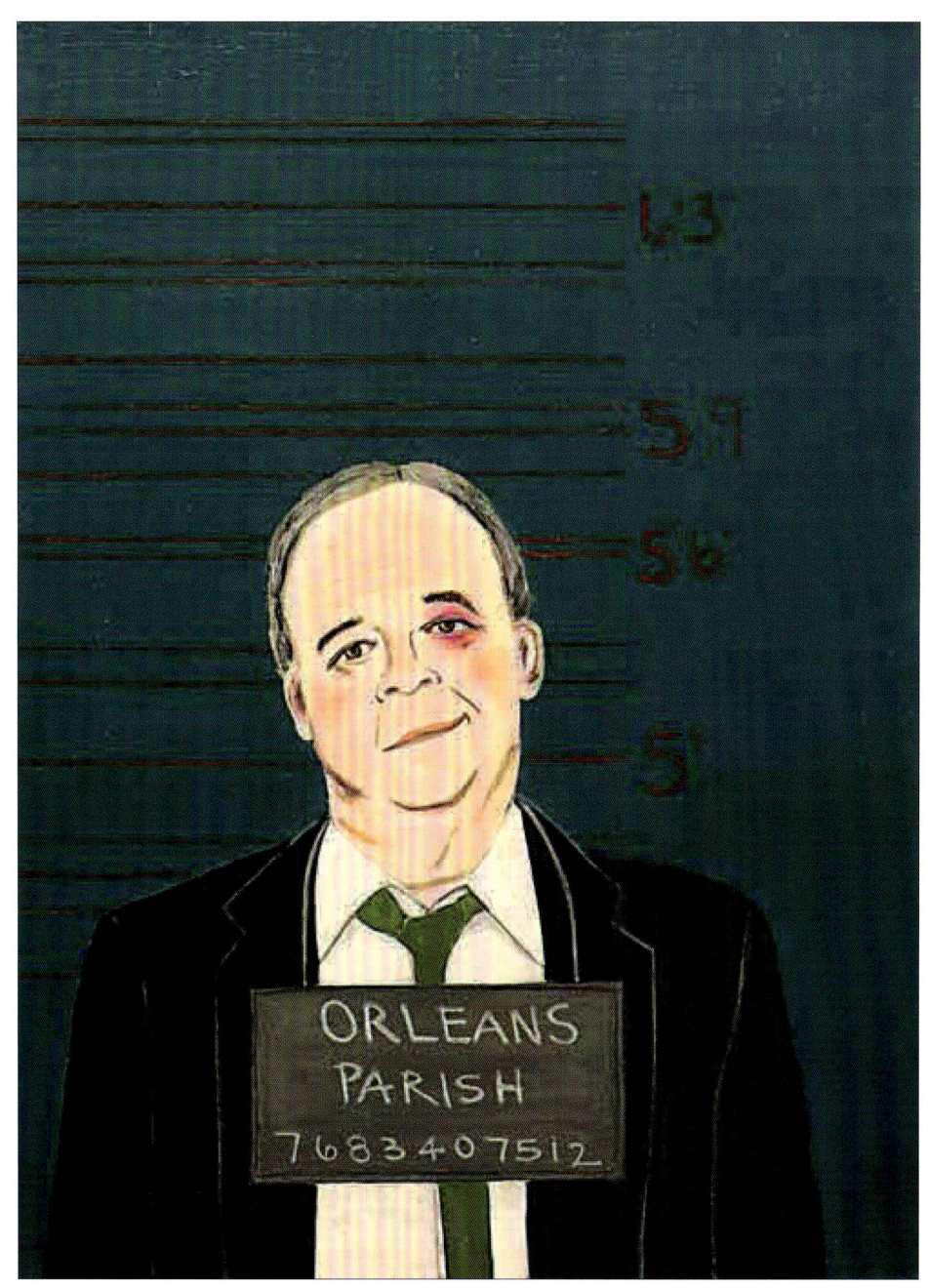

The Devil Made Me Do it   48" x 36"   acrylic on canvas

DAVE GREBER

Philadelphia, Pennsylvania, 1982

OUR PHYSICAL SELF IS NEVER SOLELY A matter of biology. According to Carl Jung, our Persona, the mask we show the world, has always been a matter of intent, of projection. It's a process of individuation integrating the conscious and unconscious with a battalion of archetypes slithering their way up through the collective. With contemporary digital extensions, our personas have now entered into a terrain of avatars, screen names, and identities assumed for on-line dating and social networking. According to Dave Greber, *NanoSwarm Projections* "attempts to unify these spirits into a new composite entry and personify them." In preparing his *NanoSwarm* videos, Gerber shoots ten to twenty "first-world, 21st Century humans" in front of a green screen, each going through the same emotions and expressions. Using mattes and a painted background, a kinetic, multi-leveled portrait is formed, a new digital composite of personas projected into yet another digital reality. Born in Philadelphia, Greber studied media production before moving to New Orleans, where he began producing videos. In 2009 he began to create site-specific video installations as well as video commentaries that broke down the language of corporate propaganda with skeleton "commercials" built from the tone, cadence, verbal and graphic illusions that comprise a corporate campaign. In "PumpkinPencil™ by SquashScribe ®," Greber attempts to take what he calls the "parasitic language" of television commercials and covert it to "viewer empowerment" by making the commercialized product and the means to market it absurd. A series of actors in a studio environment sell a preposterous product with a catalog of promises and corporate spin slogans in endless loop. The hypnotic manipulations of commercialism are employed to objectives which border somewhere between a Saturday Night Live sketch and an authentic commercial experience, enabling a viewer to question their participation in a free-market commercialized system.

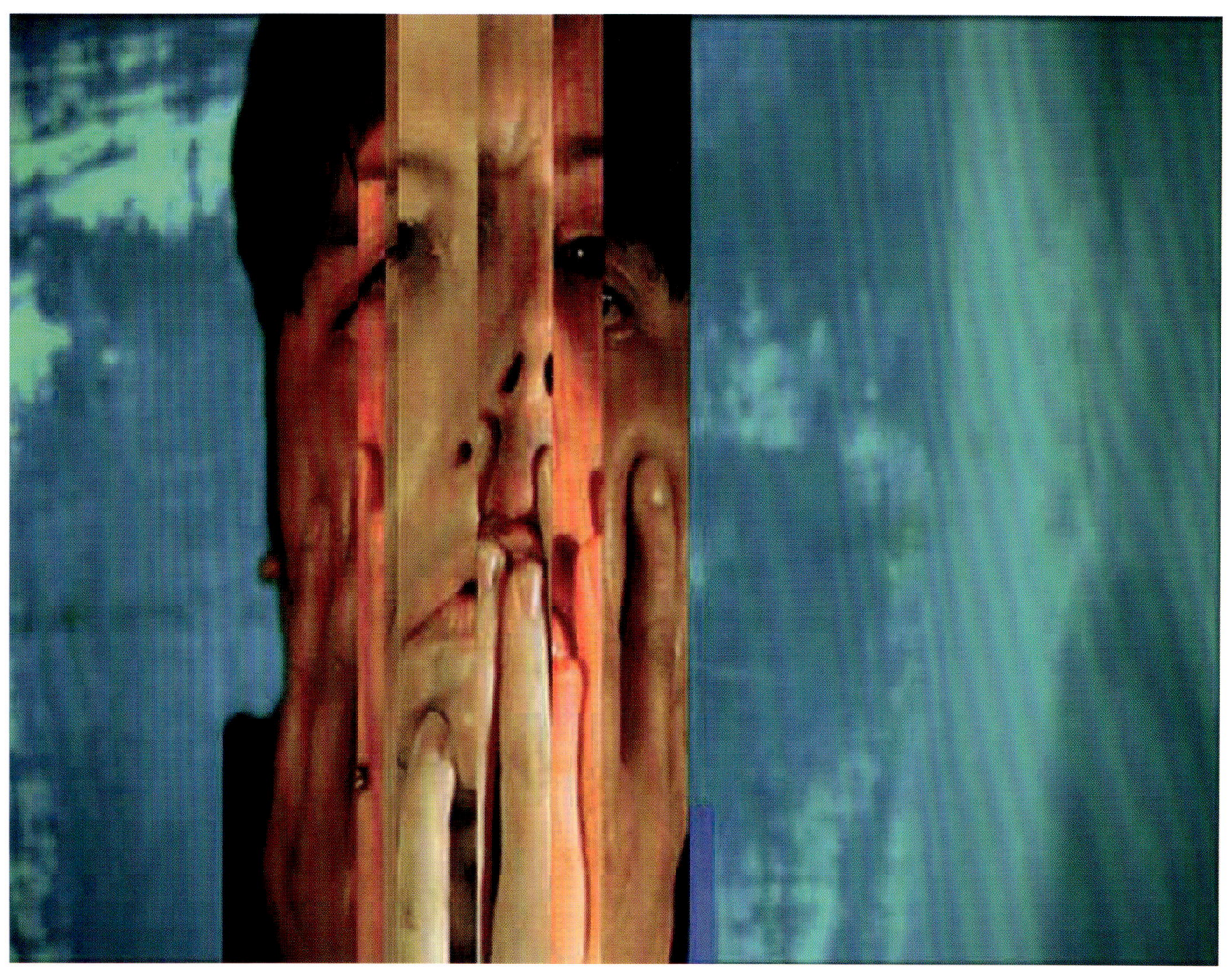

Faces from the NanoSwarm Projections   running time: 44:33   video

GRISSEL GIULIANO

Hartford, Connecticut, 1976

DEATH – SINCE ITS EXPERIENCE IS INEXorably bound to this side of things – is life. It is not life's negation but exists within life's continuum. How else do we calculate loss, absence, even decay if not with the vocabulary of the living? We know nothing of death, which is why art is in charge of its representation, and has made many an investigation: Jacques-Louis David's *Death of Marat*, Edvard Munch's *Sickroom*, the ecstatic horrors of Bosch, Klimt's *Death and Life*, Waterhouse's drowned *Ophelia*, just to name a few. We've got Hamlet contemplating the firmament and grave, Ingmar Bergman's black-robed scepter-wielding and chess-playing specter, and Damien Hirst's vivisections. All of these representations are merely our way of gazing through the glass onion. Art is always life, even while addressing death. Art asks: What does death look like? And: Why does it not look enough like death? Grissel Giuliano has photographed a series of dead chicks and found death wanting. The death she found was not nothingness, but somethingness; a dance of poses that does not demand to be buried, but instead invites one to extend a finger to tickle its still-cute fur. The viewer understands they are not looking at a living bird (nor a representation of a living bird), but the ghoulish playfulness that death sometimes lends itself. It could be like laughing at the brain-munching undead of countless movies, which amuse Giuliano among the many. Giuliano's death is a curio, like the peeled and posed of the *Bodies* exhibitions, or Damien Hirst's lambs and sharks in vitrines of formaldehyde. Giuliano demonstrates that no subject is off limits to art. Death belongs to art as much as to the mortician or the clergy. Art, in fact, owns those, too.

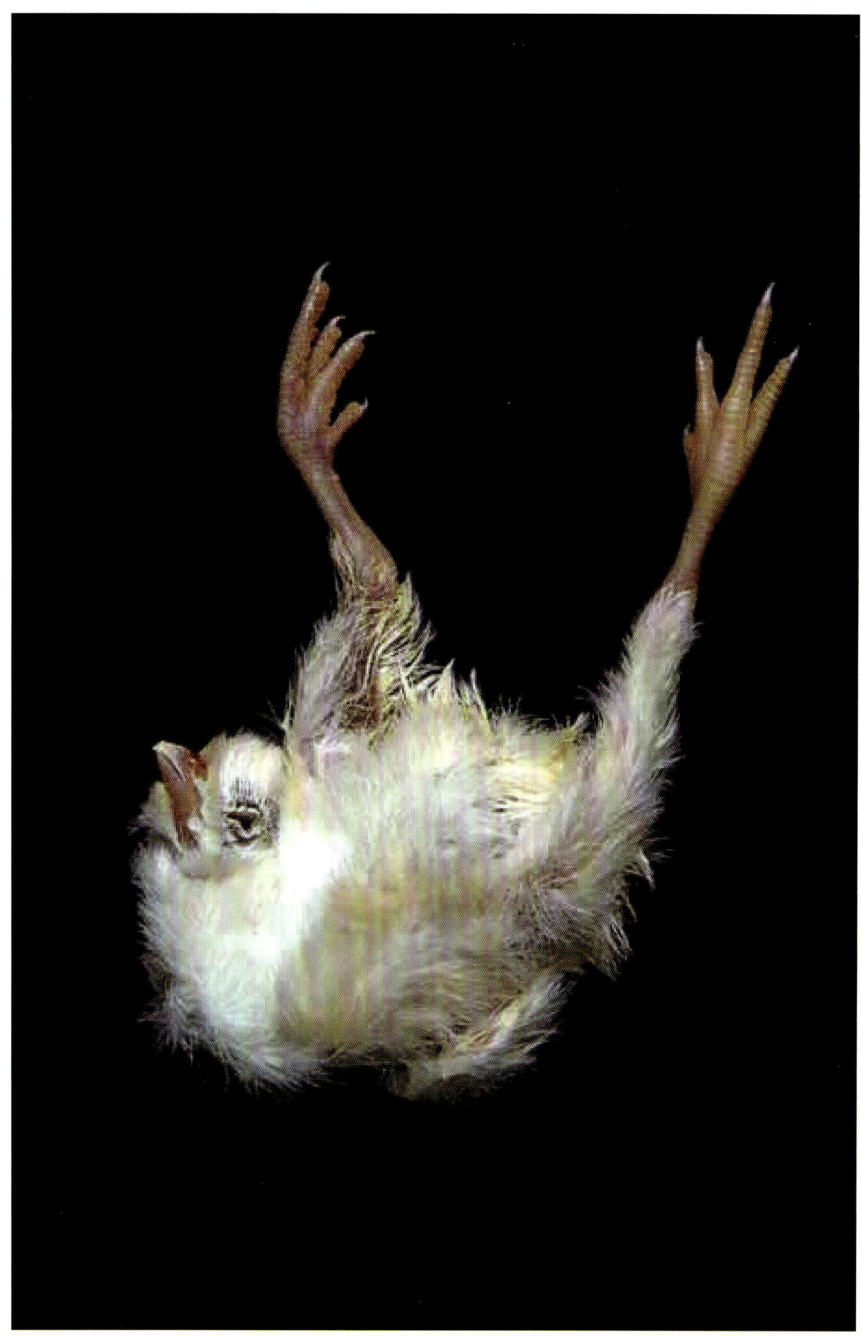

Chick Study 10   60" x 40"   archival color photograph

NICK HASSLOCK

New Orleans, Louisiana, 1982

FROM THE 1880'S THROUGH THE 1920'S, blue-lettered white tiles identifying street names were installed into the cross-walks city-wide. Those original tiles were cast in Alhambra, Spain, and imported into New Orleans by an American company, which went bankrupt when the stock market crashed in 1929. Since then, natural decay, the great roots of proud Live Oaks, and the electrical workers of Entergy have been steadily destroying the tiles. Nick Hasslock, the son of ceramicists, was approached by a New Orleans city civil engineer for a recommendation on who might be capable of recreating the tiles. Hasslock proposed himself and earned the commission. Thus far Hasslock has cast 3,000 tiles, replacing those throughout the Midcity, Garden District, and Bywater neighborhoods. Each individual tile is slipcast in a plastic mold with its signature blue letter syringed directly into it while heating. The craftsmanship and patience of Hasslock's work attracted *Saratoga Collection* curator Terrence Sanders as Sanders sought an artisan to create the Hurricane Katrina memorial, which was to be included into the Saratoga Building. The memorial will include the names of the 1,830 documented victims of Hurricane Katrina. Composed of several conjoined pieces of granite, each name is sandblasted by Hasslock and will be mounted onto a wall outside the Saratoga Building.

THIS MURAL IS DEDICATED TO THE VICTIMS OF HURRICANE KATRINA.
WE WILL FORGIVE BUT WE WILL NEVER FORGET.

CREATED BY TERRENCE SANDERS FOR 'THE SARATOGA COLLECTION' WITH THE SUPPORT OF MARCEL WISZNI

Hurricane Katrina Memorial   11' x 11'   granite

OLIVIA HILL

Hinsdale, Illinois, 1985

WHETHER PAINTING IS DEAD, INJURED, or standing well within shiny patent-leather Mary Janes, there will always be a place in the permanently-contemporary art scene for the whimsically imaginative, where the human terrain is infused with the symbolically and engagingly fantastic. Having spent her formative years in Hollywood-styled Southern California, Hill has carried to the American South a tradition of imagined time and place, a world of fairy tale illustrations with the fanfare of Gustav Klimt. Marked by a rich saturation of color, her paintings are a collage of the human and ornamental, imbued with the theatrics of situation and costume. The decorative made flesh, as in *A Dress for Mum and Babies*, echoes Egon Schiele; but unlike Schiele, Hill's figures are never solitary. Their pleasure principle requires the joyful indulgence of participation sometimes but not necessarily human. In the tradition of Lewis Carroll and past-era Disney animation, Hill grants her humans company both animal and flora, anima and animus. The faces of the figures in *We're All Mad as Apples Here* are replaced by apples, yet the characters dance in a lush field of fallen golden leaves, costumed in sequined ball-gowns and pantaloons. As is the right and rite of art, utterly absent are limitations. *Barnacle* is pure Pre-Raphaelite. Peacock-feather-etched silk pillows, a fascination with fabric folds, and sumptuous human skin give way to mythology in partial transformation towards the flesh of a sea creature. While lending her vision to the art and wardrobe departments of film and television productions shooting in the South, Hill currently is at work on *Carnival Mamou*, a collection of oil and pastel depictions of the somewhat clandestine Cajun Mardi Gras celebrations that take place in the rural towns of Louisiana.

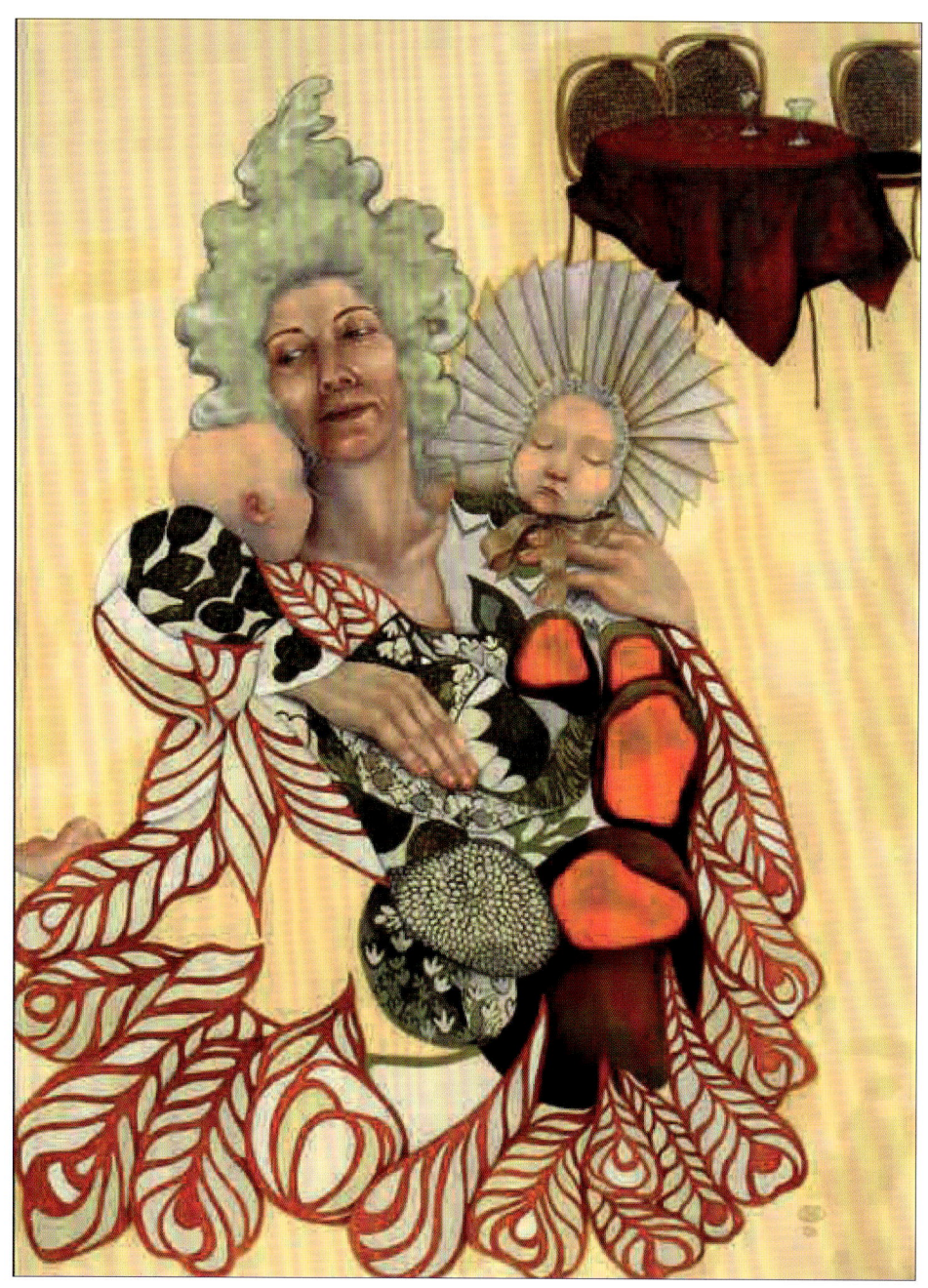

A Dress for Mum and her Babies   30" x 40"   oil on canvas

KEVIN H. JONES

Huntsville, Alabama, 1969

THE CONCEPTUAL INVESTIGATION OF THE natural world through charts, diagrams, and systems is a constant theme of Kevin H. Jones's work. Jones makes use of cameras and computer programs that do useful tasks like tracing the development of cloud charts using primitive techniques that harness energy. He places manmade systems in organic systems that include typography on leaves. Other work utilizes solar energy to power a fictional television station, and incorporates sensors to create an interactive video installation that questions entropy. In Muybridge-like grid presentations, Jones studies the progression of a snail over a small space for 396 frames, while another details the extinguishing of a candle's flame. Here Jones is providing us a framework of life on the minutest level, in almost humanly imperceptible increments. Painting, video, computing, and two-dimensional digital prints are all components of his work. Jones's piece *Hunter* includes a drawing of a person in a dog costume, an illustration of a snake, and a blurred astronomical chart. Here is a balance of relationships of natural order. The "acted" dog serves as a metaphor for a human inability to comprehend nature on an instinctual level, while the snake serves as a reference to the books from which knowledge is derived--our empirical experience which, according to Jones, is unfortunately obtained through textbooks. Jones's graphic sensibilities dictates that the heavens are beyond us, yet we are able to attempt order, endeavor to create a sense of harmony from our confusion, and utilize scientific knowledge as a bridge towards organic comprehension. Art, for Jones, is that attempt.

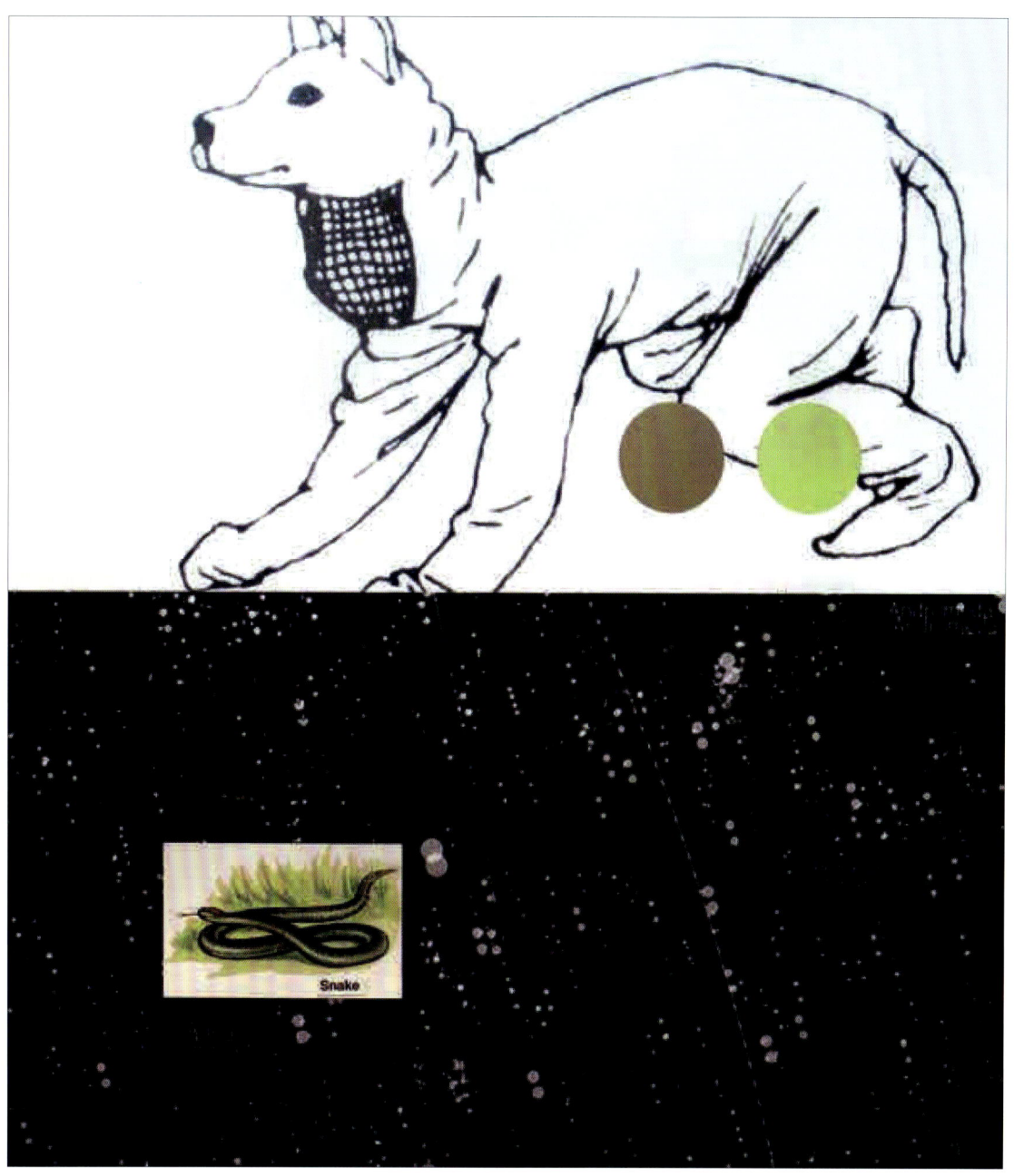

Hunter   42" x 42"   photograph mounted on aluminum

BARBIE L' HOSTE

New Orleans, Louisiana, 1981

BARBIE L'HOSTE'S CANVASES AND PAINTED porcelain slabs serve as prismatic lenses into the weird wonders of a Technicolor childhood. Sentiments of nostalgia and lost innocence are some of the purveying emotions in the multi-layered dreamscapes that contain both adult yearning and juvenescent astonishment. Utilizing collage techniques, L'Hoste color-copies figures found in vintage storybooks and encyclopedias, then shrinks, enlarges, or revises their orientation to be placed, diorama-like, into fantastic scenes of narrative indeterminate, yet suggestive enough to trigger emotional states nearly intra-uterine. The assemblage of children and figurine adults evokes the panoramas of Henry Darger, while the layering and kinetic juxtaposing bares comparison to Terry Gilliam's animation work for Monty Python. L'Hoste uses collage to build up the landscape. Fabrics, bits of wall paper, wrapping paper, and mesh netting materials provide texture and manage to tickle sensations associated with near infancy. In the painting, *I don't let it bother me, do you let it bother you?* L'Hoste combines her signature found figures in an environment that defies reason and physical limitations. The air is filled with flying ships and sea pigs (one of the most scientifically unknown and abundant deep-dwelling sea creatures). There are dancing spuds and an odd adult figure tossing plush creatures for the amusement (or perhaps need) of the children far below. The painted landscape is lush, with fat brushstrokes of child-safe colors filling in skies, seas, and cliffs, all of which securely support the children. Safety is key in these works. If there is menace, as there occasionally is in L'Hoste's work (as there is in most every fairytale), the children contained within do not sense it. Vulnerability is also their fortification, which would be a slightly unsettling paradox were it not also this mix that makes L'Hoste's works so appealing.

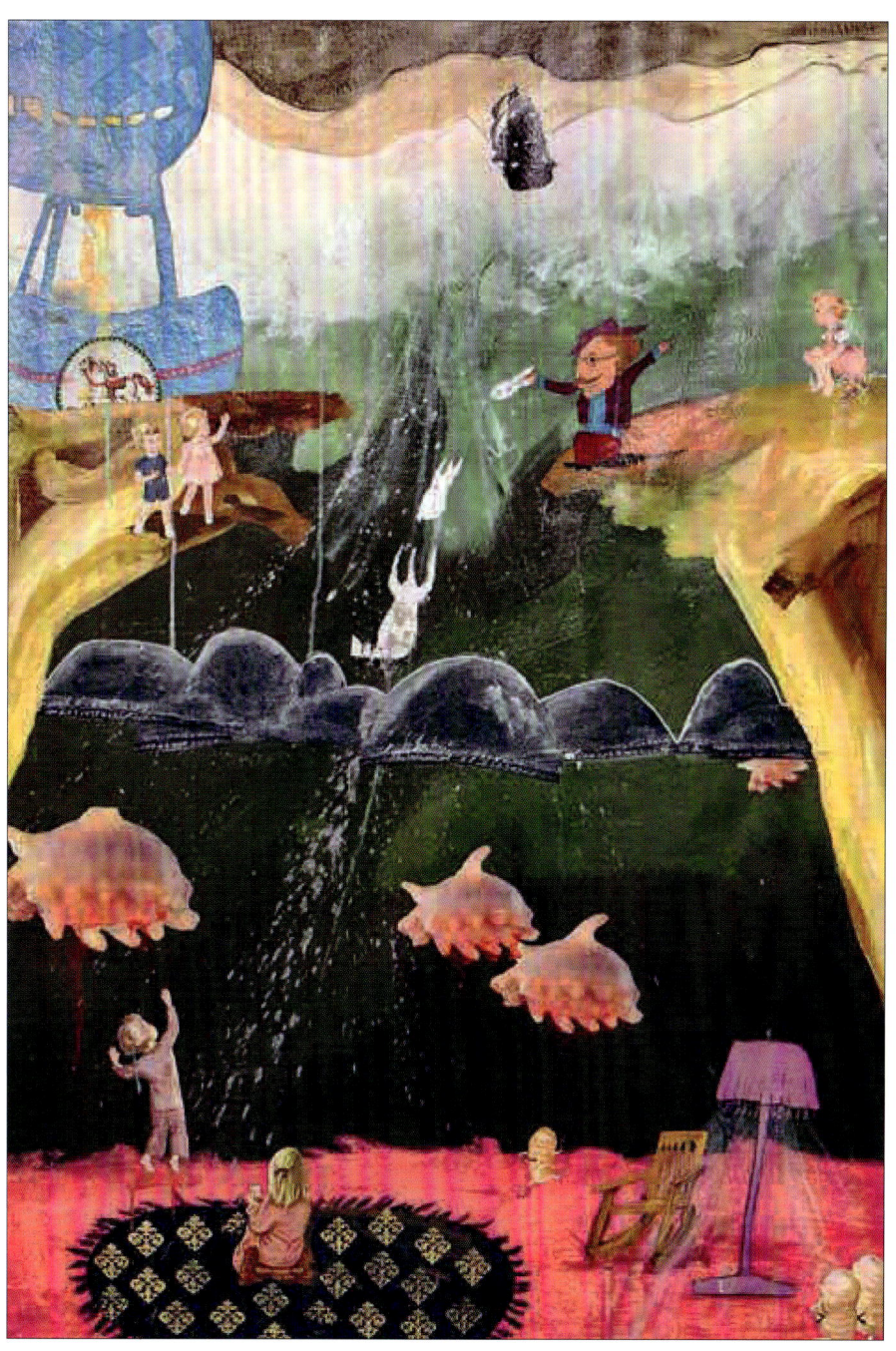

I don't let it bother me, do you let it bother you?   60" x 41"   acrylic and mixed media on canvas

CHRIS JAHNCKE

New Orleans, Louisiana, 1972

IN PETER GREENAWAY'S FILM, *DROWNING by Numbers*, the Skipping Girl counts and names the stars, and perhaps that's a wise way to approach the whimsical constellations that comprise Chris Jahncke's drawn and collage-assembled compositions. With exuberance and surreal playfulness, Jahncke combines abstraction and figuration into a stratosphere of tiny details assembled into dynamic systems. In a dance between order and chaos, Jahncke shuffles between the micro and the macro: what's to be found upon closer examination, and what's to be experienced from afar. He is interested in patterns, repetitions, and collage. Jahncke's imaginative bio-and geo-morph drawings collect into a stew of space. An accusation of clutter can be made, and Jahncke's acknowledges that parts of his assemblages are gathered recycled scraps from off the studio floor; but layering for Jahncke becomes an act of geological excavation for the viewer. Where we seek the recognizable, a parody of Euclidian forms stare back; we seek the heavens and the heavens stare down, as in Percy Shelley's "Hymn to Apollo":

> The sleepless hours who watch me as I lie,
> Curtained with star-inwoven tapestries
> From the broad moonlight of the sky,
> Fanning the busy dreams from my dim eyes.

Jahncke's *Mental Scraps* is a creation of stream-of-conscious, Pollock-like impulse and process where drips are replaced with forms related to biology and archetypal symbols, anything that came to mind when the brush and pen hit the paper. Jahncke's works evoke Miro, Klee, certainly Jean Dubuffets' Hourloupes, as well as Hundertwasser's bright colors, organic forms, a rejection of the straight line, and the reconciliation of human and geological nature.

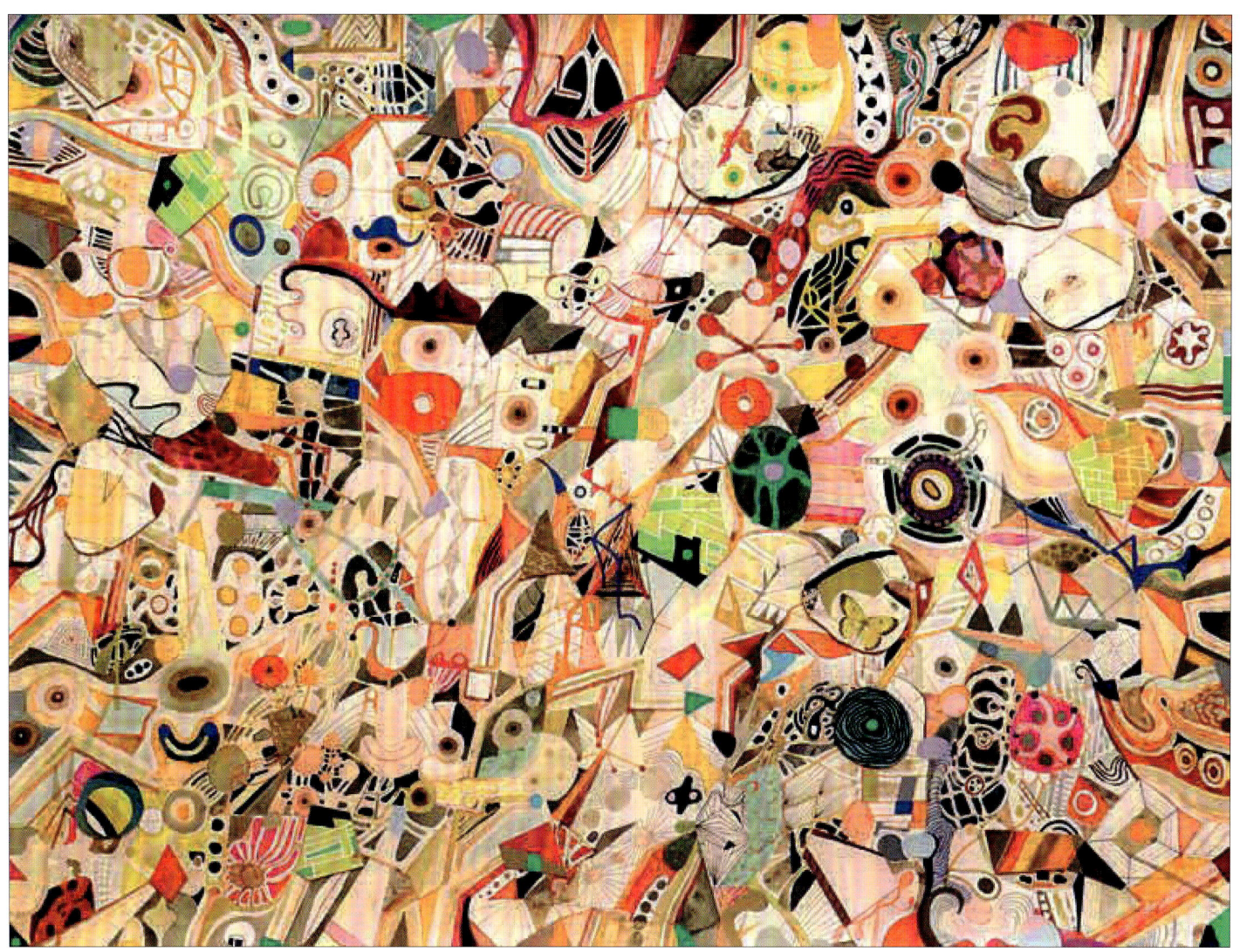

Mental Scraps   22" x 30"   mixed media on paper

BRUCE KEYES

New Orleans, Louisiana, 1950

WHILE SERVING IN THE U.S. NAVY, ON A TOUR of Vietnam from 1969-1971, Bruce Keyes traveled throughout East Asia taking photographs with his first camera. The survey of an overseas experience leant him the confidence to return to New Orleans as a working photographer. In his near forty years of experience, Keyes has taken on several surveys, his black and white photographs comprising *Spirit of New Orleans* being the most notable. This iconic collection, which comprises thirty years of Mardi Gras parades, second-line funeral marches, Jazz Fest, and street musicians as well as a plentitude of daily New Orleans moments, comprises a book as well as two separate solo exhibitions, one at the Center for the Study of Southern Culture at the University of Mississippi, the other within the George and Leah McKenna Museum of African American Art in New Orleans. Equally as significant as the particular rendering of New Orleans spectacles are the faces of the individuals which fill them. Rarely does one of Keyes's images fail to provide a singular, and often unexpected, expression: the momentous intent of a performing saxophonist, the rapture of revelers, the discarded sorrows of working class men who have been chosen to don honored Mardi Gras costumes. It is this investigation into human nature and the meaning of expression, gesture, and timing that Keyes brought to his *Weapons of Choice* series, of which "Tatiania" is part. Keyes invited an open forum of individuals to be photographed brandishing their favorite weapons. He shot thirty individuals in full figure before an enormous American flag. While the study deals with individual fascination with weaponry in today's society, specifically in America with its diehard-grip on the Second Amendment, there is a duality to the meaning of weaponry in this urban, violent, and yet ethereal image. Leaning into the phalanx of a lily is Tatania, with her foreign-sounding name, turning, finally, away from a cycle of violence and towards nature, or is she commenting that nature itself is an innate component of human aggression? Keyes provides no definite answer, indicating only that to stand empty-handed before the stars and stripes is not an option.

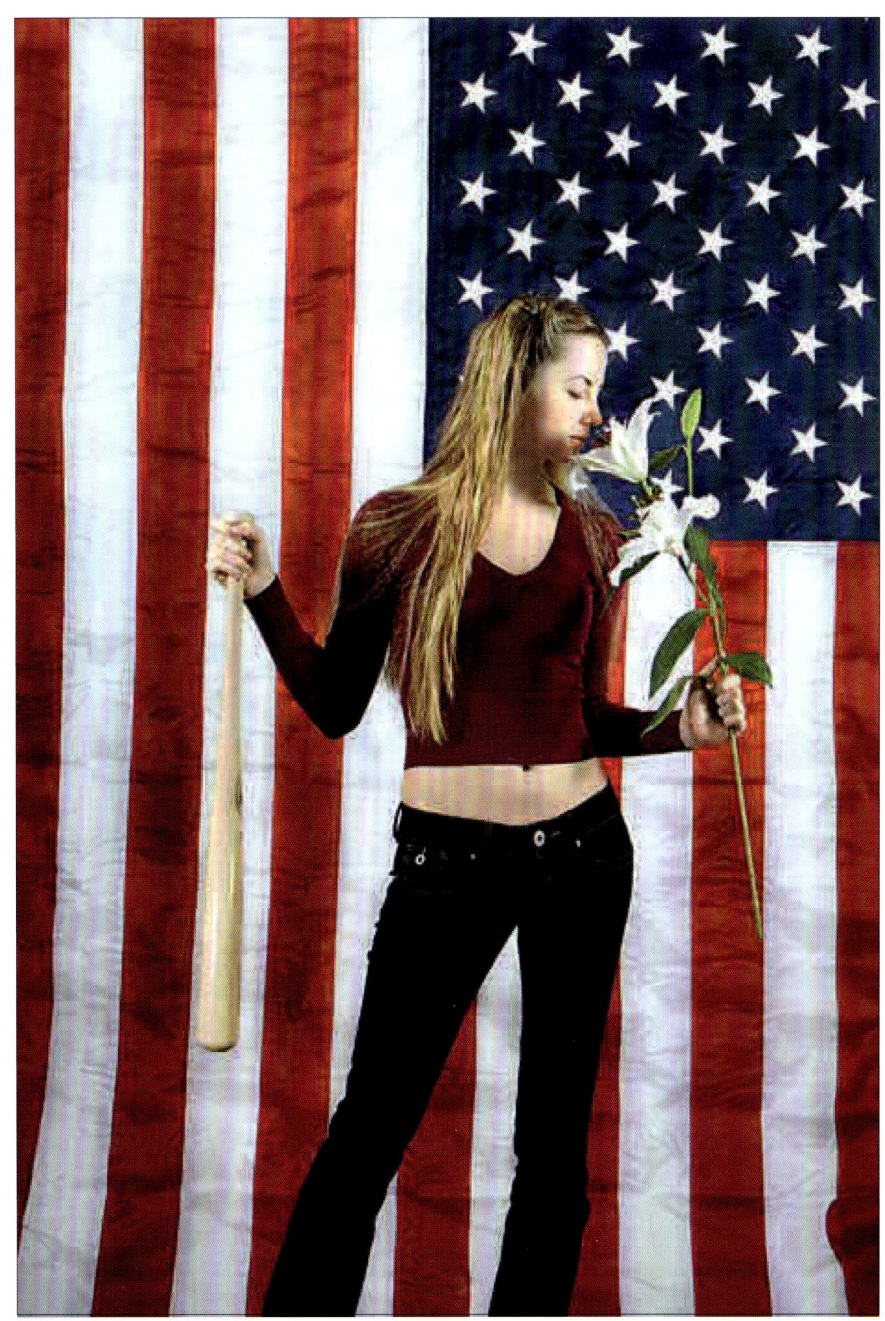

Tatiania   36" x 24"   color photograph on archival rag paper

STEPHEN KWOK

Bartlesville, Oklahoma, 1987

EVERY IPHONE, DROID, BLACKBERRY, AND other unnamed, soon-to-be-obsolete Personal Digital Assistant has a To-Do List application. This post-post-industrial age (if that's where we are) still recognizes that humanity needs such lists. The invention of the Post-It Note served as the ultimate papyrus for the To-Do list. Lily Tomlin devised her character Trudy as a bag lady so covered in to-do lists that a decent breeze might have blown them away, leaving us to find her bodiless. Individuals, communities, entire societies can be compartmentalized into To-Do lists, at least that's what Stephen Kwok seems to present with his *To-Do Lists: New Orleans*. Kwok sent a task force of twenty to hit up random people in various New Orleans neighborhoods and asked them to write a to-do list for the rest of their day. Afterwards, Kwok colleted the lists and taped them into a clean grid onto a wall as a sort of memorial. Where most memorials stand to commemorate calamities, though, Kwok's wall, like the to-do list itself, stands in for something much more fleeting, transient, and bound to the blink-of-the-moment. What is on the lists? Someone probably scribbled: Pick up milk, while another might have scribed: Don't forget to believe in God. In each list there is the writer's individuation and a conceptualization of his or her collection, which stands in for society itself; it's needs, desires, and self-identification. Other "projex" of Kwok's include having individuals write open letters to their arch-nemeses, which Kwok posted in long tassel strands on telephone poles in the New Orleans Bywater neighborhood. He has also projected questions such as: *What If You're Not So Special* on gallery walls, played word games by applying single words onto a collection of protective eye-goggle lenses, and made other lists, including his "Incurable Appreciation," a Top-100 Influencers which gathers Confucius, Coco Chanel, and Christopher Columbus (just to stay with the Cs), and that includes their fabricated average annual income and net worth at death. Hijincks, conceptual forays, individual and societal inquiry: art.

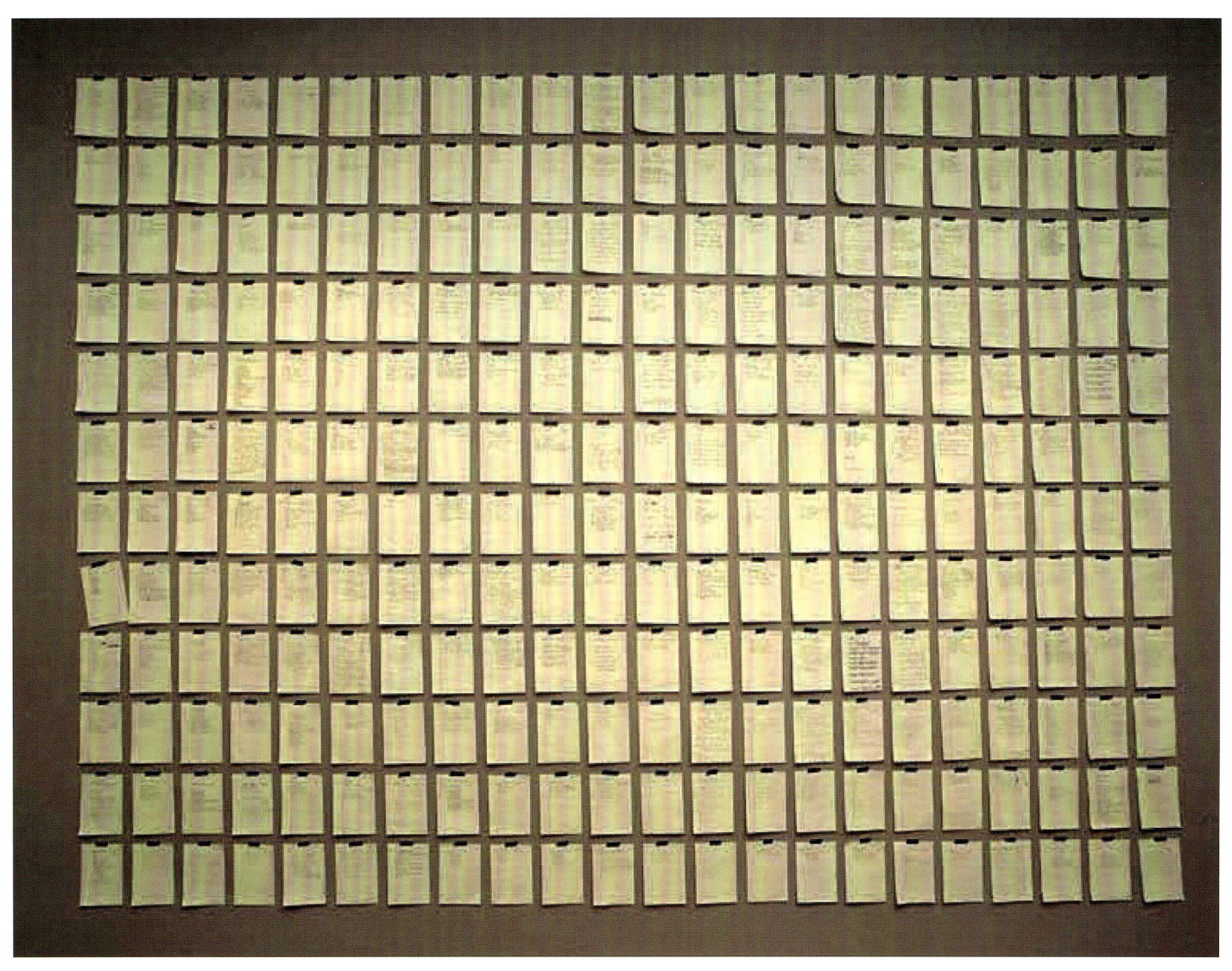

To Do Lists: New Orleans   80" x 120"   mixed media on paper mounted on acid free foam core

MIRANDA LAKE

Norwalk, Connecticut, 1969

OUR COLLECTIVE VISUAL AND LITERARY investigations of animal-human syllogistic relationships is nearly limitless. Is it a matter of imagination, or simply envy for what our bodies will never obtain? To defy gravity, live in sky and breathe underwater, to run with gazelle velocity. Miranda Lake carries on the investigation with cabinets of curiosity that harvest the insect and animal kingdom into landscapes inescapably altered by human intervention. She assembles encaustic collages of found objects and photographs that are sealed in a pigmented beeswax, an art-making technique dating back to ancient Greece. Wax has long been a substance for the collection and physical preservation of insects. It was also the sealing agent that bound the feathers of Icarus's wings, which both allowed him flight and ultimately sealed his fate. The Icarus association seems apt to Lake's work. In *Refinery*, from *Lake's reclamation:360˚* series, a flutter of luminous butterflies cling, as if feeding, to the cooling and exhaust towers of an industrial refinery. While humanity is reliant on technology to make up for our physical insufficiencies, nature in Lake's work snuggles up to our machines, our industries. In "this could be the ride of our lives" Lake makes exploration of the landscape surrounding New Orleans as the flora and fauna reclaimed the Katrina-ravaged Gulf Coast. Here birds encircle the undulating steel of a rollercoaster, detritus from the Six Flags amusement park, that remained underwater (as if sealed in beeswax) for a month following the destruction of Hurricane Katrina. The ride, which sees no more human visitors, has become ornithological property. By combining human industry with animal fortitude, Lake's work anthropomorphizes the animal kingdom while acknowledging our own primordial resources.

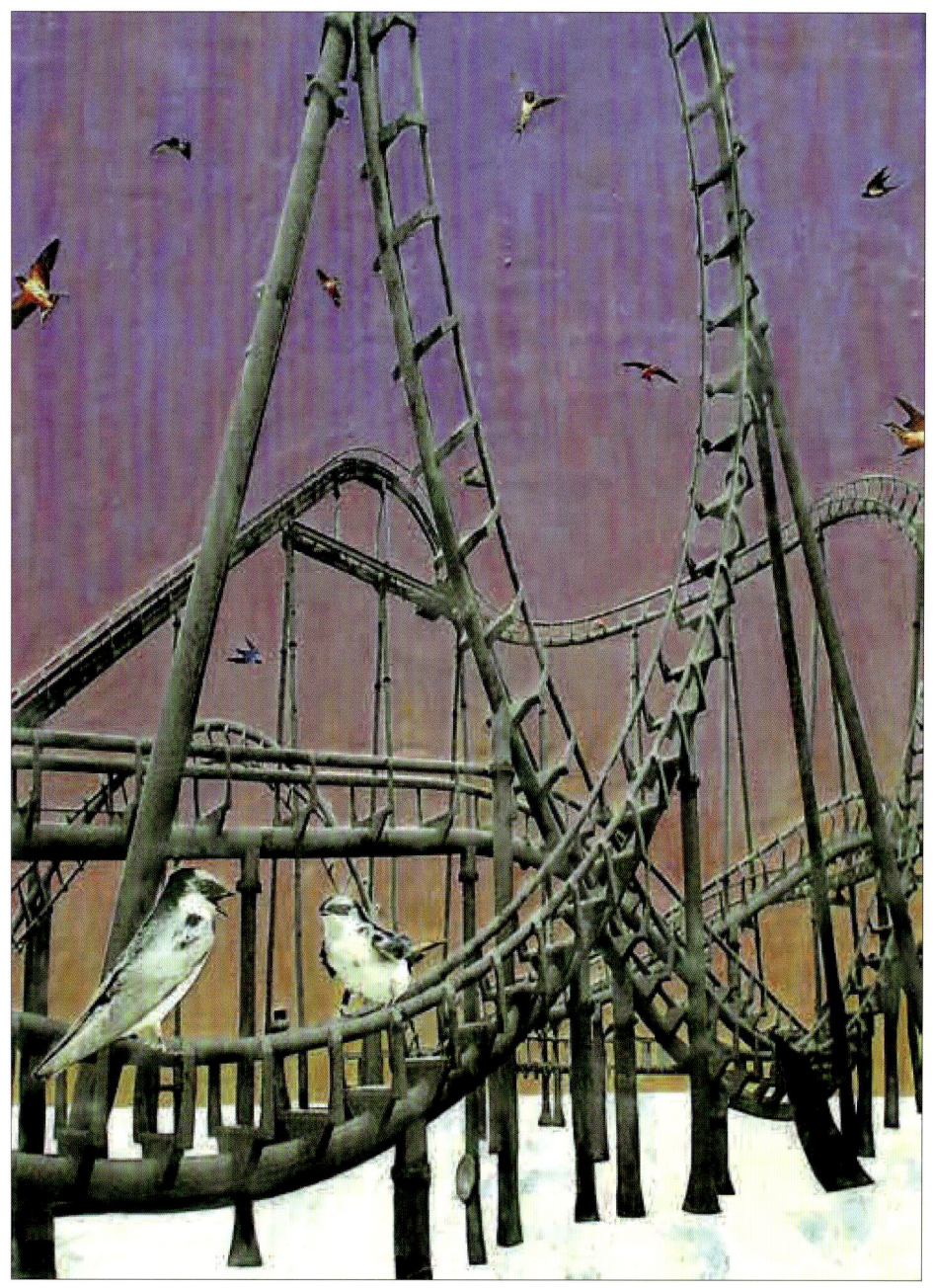

This Could be the Ride of Our Lives 40" x 30" encaustic collage on canvas

SRDJAN LONCAR

Rijeka, Croatia, 1971

SRDJAN LONCAR'S *FIX-A-THING* PROJECT involves going out into the world to repair damaged objects with close-up photographic images of those objects. In *Fix-a-thing (Bricks)* he mends a broken stoop in front of his house with photographs of bricks sculpted to Styrofoam shaped like bricks. Loncar is cavalier with camera settings. If the camera picks up a blue tone due to lighting, then that is what the sculpture (because that is what the fixed thing becomes) is made of. Included in the Saratoga Collection is an archival inkjet-on-aluminum print of *Fix-a-thing (Deer)*, in which Loncar renovates a pair of (fake) deer antlers with rods and foam covered with photographs of deer antlers. We take a steep step down the recess of representation when we represent a thing with a representation of the thing which the thing represents. But Loncar's theoretical intent also remains on surface level (albeit perhaps skating the surface upside-down) when he suggests that his *Fix-a-things* might also act as fast-patch duct tape solutions for our crumbling environs. Practical or not, the mixing of near-utilitarian function with artistic intent makes Borges-games of everyday experience. It is the Photoshoping of real life. The representational replaces the real with an approximation that only slightly exaggerates its functional impermanence. Loncar's featured Prospect.1 project involved creating a bank of fake-money sculptures installed at the Old New Orleans U.S. Mint. The historical precedence of currency printing combined conceptually with a demonstration of value as tellers offered sales of the sculpted money for investors to take home. Also shown during Prospect.1 was Loncar's *Burning Hummer*, a toy car spouting an inferno of flames made from the images of burning oil wells in Iraq. Here Loncar managed to fuse consumer consumption with environmental cost, illustrating the power of art as socio/political commentary while maintaining aesthetic and spectacle.

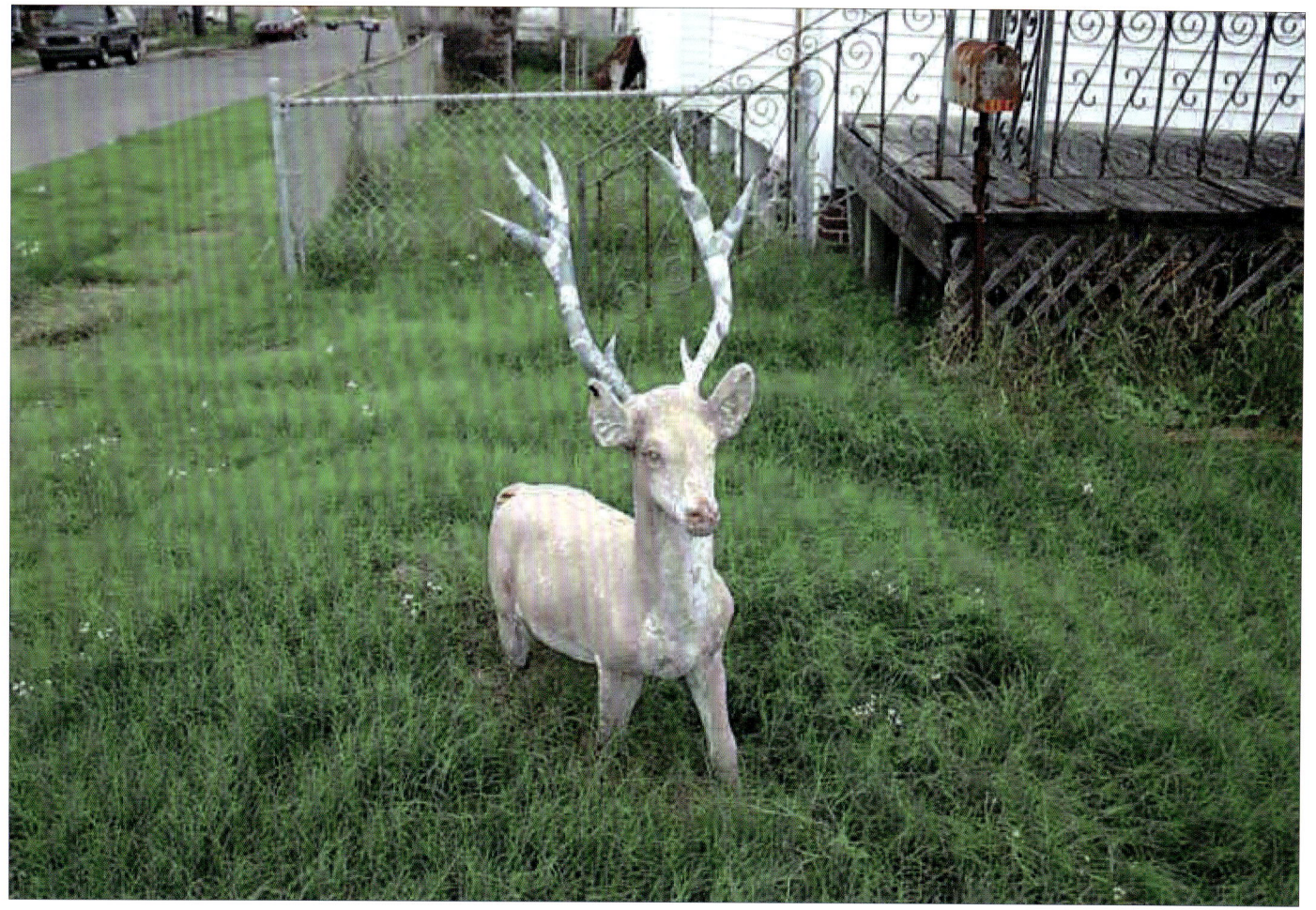

Fix-a-thing (Deer)   23" x 25"   archival inkjet on aluminum

COLIN MENEGHINI

New Orleans, Louisiana, 1982

COLIN MENEGHINI'S PAINTING *CARROLLTON Junction (Story of Tyrone)*, describes the homeless habitation of man named Tyrone who once resided beneath the Carrollton Overpass near Tulane Avenue. Through the depiction of city spaces, the work manifests Tyrone's travels, travails, and marginalized displacement. In New Orleans, the swath of medians bisecting roadways are referred to as "neutral grounds," but Meneghini offers spaces which are anything but neutral. They are instead menacing, isolating. They provide commuter efficacy and neighborhood divisions, but they can also be spaces of the abandoned, their function shifted from service to basest survival. From Tyrone's perspective they become residences and places of concealment. Meneghini's canvas is a free terrain with a multiplicity of perspectives and demarcation lines, planes within planes, just as Tyrone creates a myriad of personal territories from urban vistas. The canvas studies architectural structures, but not the sort that would do an art and architecture student (which Meneghini has been) any good. Instead, the assessment of city infrastructure becomes a journey through them. Meneghini takes us on one man's passage, a Robinson Crusoe stranded among concrete and steel, where it is always twilight, and shadows provide both haven and hazard. Tyrone, like Crusoe, is alone. Instead of a footprint providing the first hint of humanity, Tyrone has the overpass, the highway billboard, and a skyline thick with electric and telephone lines. Meneghini manages to profoundly personalize the landscape; it becomes the inner-scape as well as outer. Tyrone's impasse manages to become Meneghini's guiding principle, aiming the viewer's gaze towards the overlooked, summoning a relation to spaces that are often traversed but rarely seen.

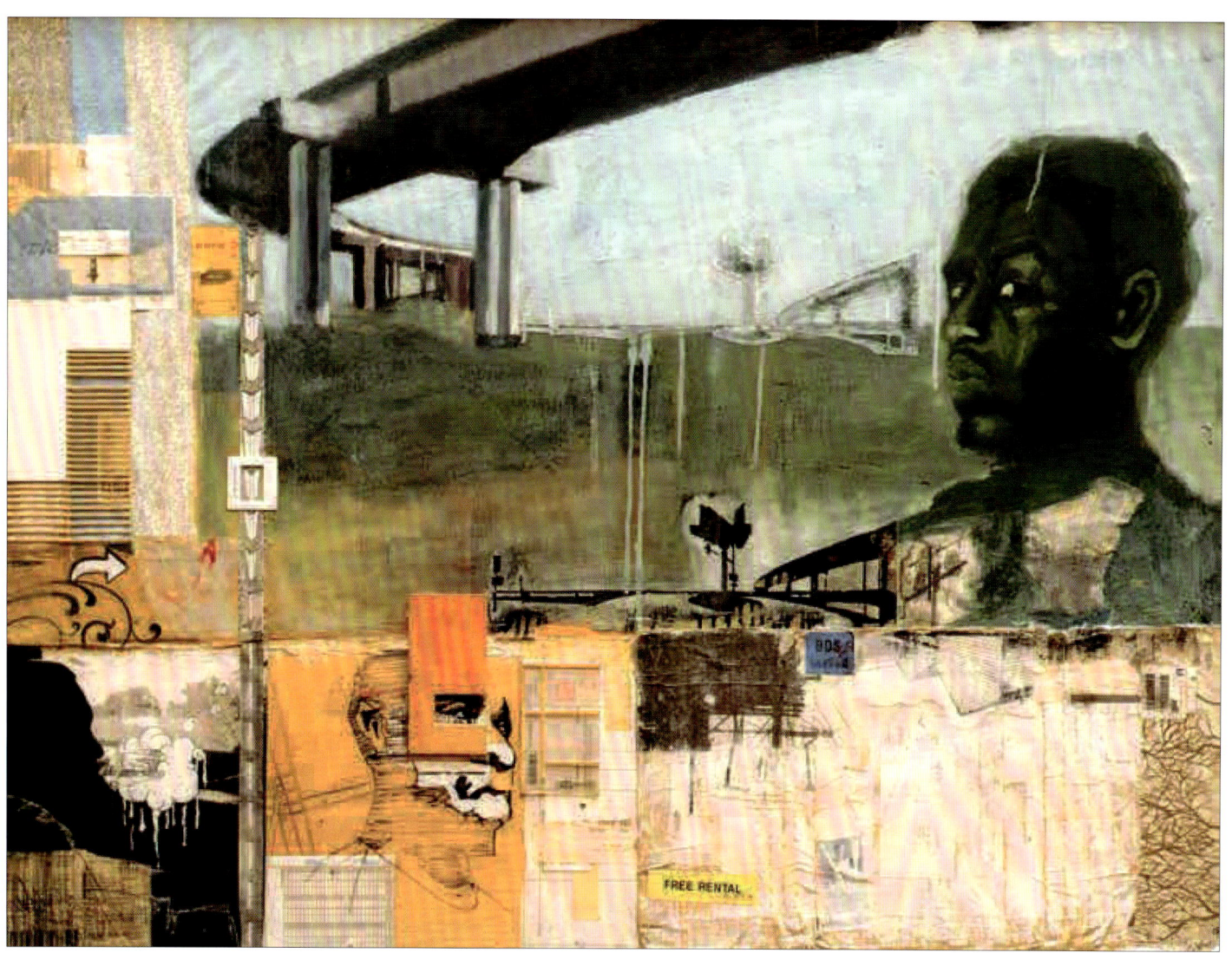

Carrollton Junction (Story of Tyrone)   36" x 48"   mixed media of wood panel

LAYLA MESSKOUB

Englewood, New Jersey, 1983

BEHIND THE FRAIL PAPERS ON WHICH LAYLA Messkoub's works are ultimately printed is the trembling enthusiasm of the child who discovers, on a Fall walk a perfectly preserved leaf transformed in color by the season and filled with a near perfect symmetrical terrain of veins. It is the type of wonder that never leaves an artist interested in the shape of things. Messkoub is concerned with textures and details, the strange living tapestry of the natural world endlessly bifurcating, spiraling, and conjoining into patterns only the trained eye can trace. Messkoub's collages incorporate hand-drawn elements as well as woodcuts that have been printed on varied papers that are then cut and reassembled. The reconstructions emphasize and reconfigure relationships and patterns and create new movements. Her woodcut collage, *Man-o-War III*, depicts the ascension of a bloom of jellyfish. If the swarm of a million spermatozoa upon a single ovum were a ballet, it would have this sort of momentum: dynamic and sensual, purposeful and potent. Messkoub studied relief printmaking at Columbia University. She has traveled extensively through Central America, Europe, and Central Asia. While textural inquiry allows Messkoub to incorporate such materials as sisal, jute, twine and human hair into her work, it is the arabesque found in birds and spotted fish, flowers, bee wings, roots, and other living matter that sets the eye a'dance. Messkoub's work possesses some of the investigations of Ernst Haeckel, though where Haeckel was a naturalist who sought to define the natural world with meticulous drawings of the plant and animal kingdom, Messkoub seeks to draw poetry from predetermined forms. A cross-pollination of living and industrial matter is at play. New conversations on what classifies the natural order of things are summoned. Just as one area of our collective imagination seeks to combine flesh with technology, so does another component maintain a morphological gaze on our biological origins, finding endless fascination in the elemental. Messkob's work belongs to the latter.

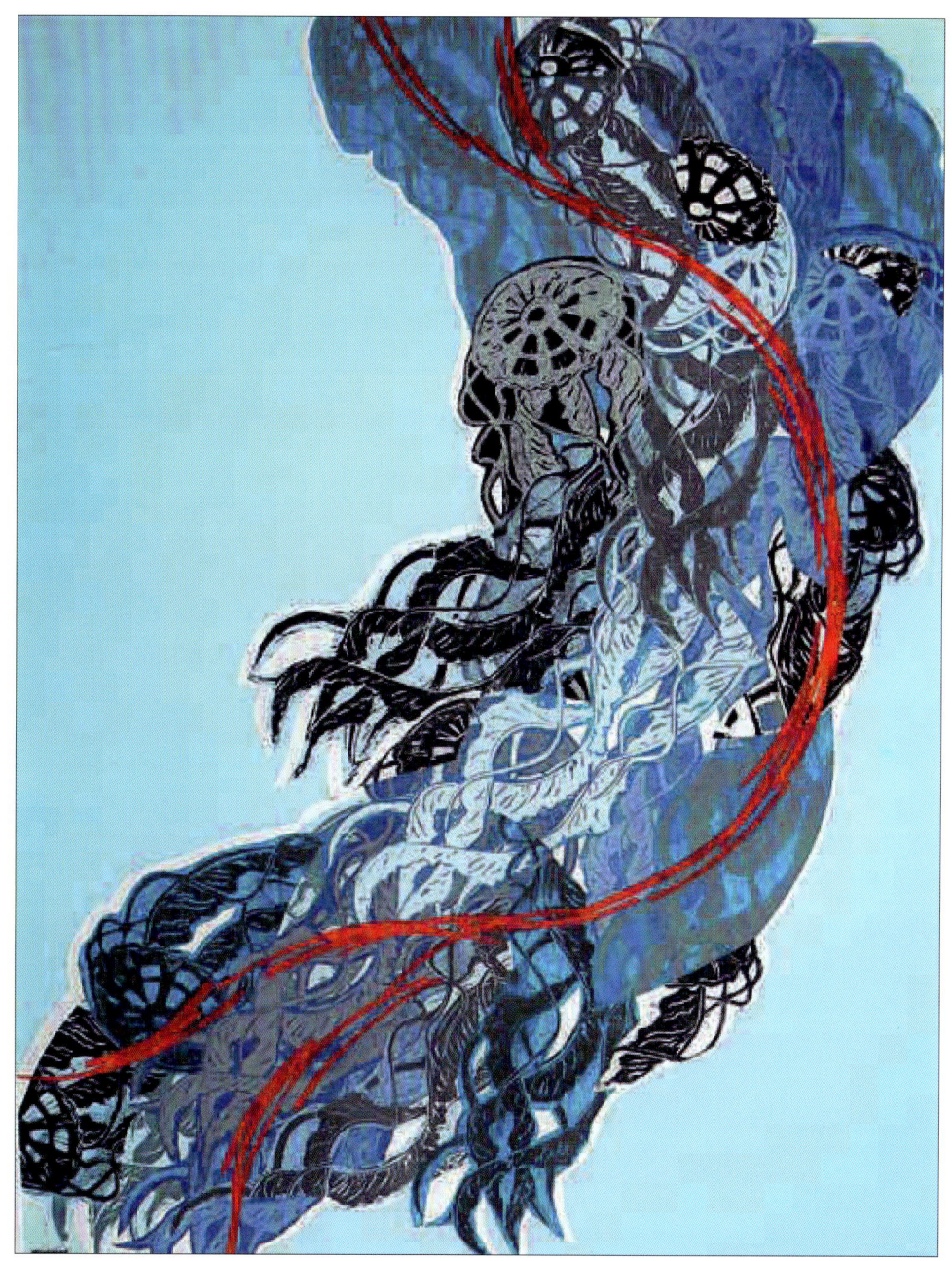

Man-o-War III   30" x 30"   woodcut collage on paper

TONY NOZERO

Detroit, Michigan, 1971

WHEN HENRI MATISSE BROUGHT A collection of African masks to Pablo Picasso's studio, he introduced the primitive into modern art, which has sustained itself from the modern through the post-modern era. Think Paul Gauguin, Jean-Michel Basquiat, Chris Ofili. The visual arts continue to be concerned with primal forms as depicted by totem shapes and strong colors, a seeking out of the pulse and raw energy contained at the source of things. Tony Nozero combines a tradition of folk and primitive paintings with New-meets-Old-world funkiness. Nozero was a long-time drummer before trading drumsticks for paintbrush. Self-taught, he paints instinctively and from that process draws forth innate shapes and human forms against a backdrop of often joyous primary colors. Nozero's painting style could be called innocent if Nozero were not so smart and if he were not also socially attuned to the decrepitude, corruption, and persistent celebration of his personal New Orleans. His painting *Stolen* was adapted from a tiny flyer he found in the streets following the devastation of Hurricane Katrina, when life in the city was still quite precarious. The painted text is a direct record of that flyer, and the child-like drawing of the car is Nozero's painterly transcription of modern technology returned, along with his city, to a state of forced chastity, lawlessness, and a ravaged but unrelenting Eden. "Usually my process isn't that obvious," Nozero says. "My usual thing is to go in there and just begin making marks until something begins to make sense. Out of frustration, or maybe just process, I'll find a path and the painting finds a way out. It usually has nothing to do with the original idea, but is a deeper version of it, more subconscious. Art can be quite liberating, and is much cheaper than a therapist."

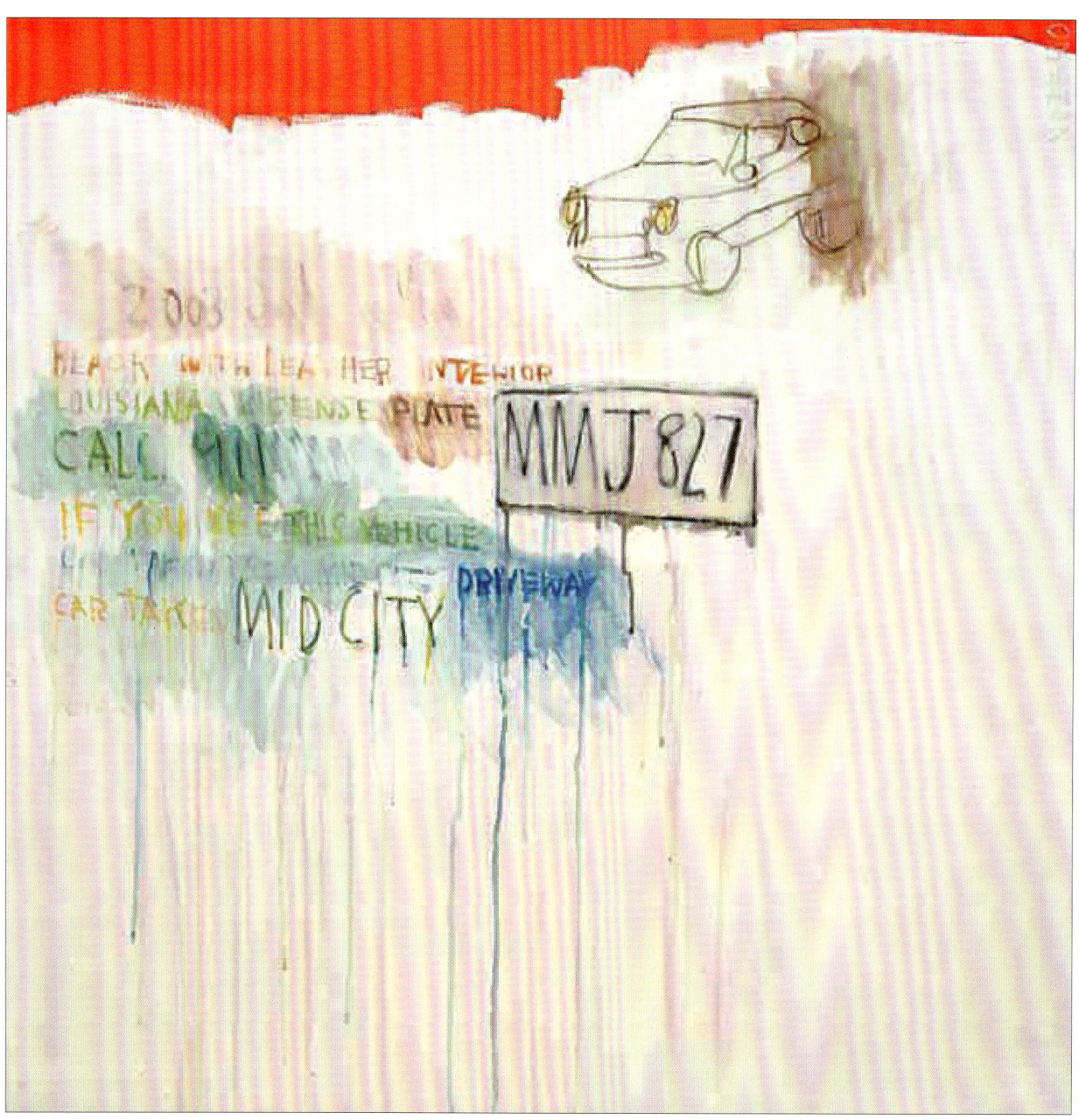

Stolen   42" x 42"   acrylic on canvas

ALEX PODESTA

Durham, North Carolina, 1973

IN HIS RECENT *SELF-PORTRAIT AS BUNNIES* series, Alex Podesta creates full-size sculptures of himself in bunny costumes. But they are more than just costumes. Podesta's is a sort of Dostoyevskian doubling, the kind that Darren Aronofsky has explored in his recent film, *Black Swan*. We are dealing with the sort of doubling that instantaneously makes its own claims, that possesses, if not life, then a projected persona that has the ability to turn itself on its creator with demands of its own. Podesta's public artwork, *City Watch*, has a tribe of five full-size Podesta-bunnies keeping watch from over the roof of the Falstaff Building in Mid City. Across the street is the New Orleans city jail. Are these child-fashioned yet adult-framed sentries eyeing for escaped convicts? Or is this an advantageous point to wait for incoming weather, storms, or future hurricanes? Having projected himself into the shape of these chimeras, Podesta brings new contextualization to the dualities of his own hybrid-being: the boy and the man; the dreamer and the creator; he who fantasizes and he who takes control. Childhood innocence and adult knowing have been fashioned into a singular form, and that form repeated. Podesta's *Self-Portrait as Bunnies (Hubris)*, has a pair of bunny-men performing surgery on a toy bunny. What is the over-weaned pride to which the "hubris" in the title refers? Have these Podesta-creations, now out to assemble their own creation, taken their evolution one step too far? On the floor beside their surgery is a mask of Podesta's face and an issue of *Art Forum*. Are these ingredients all it takes to engage in the creative process? By projecting himself into nascent self-confrontation, Podesta engages in a multifarious game of role-play before the question of audience ever enters into the equation.

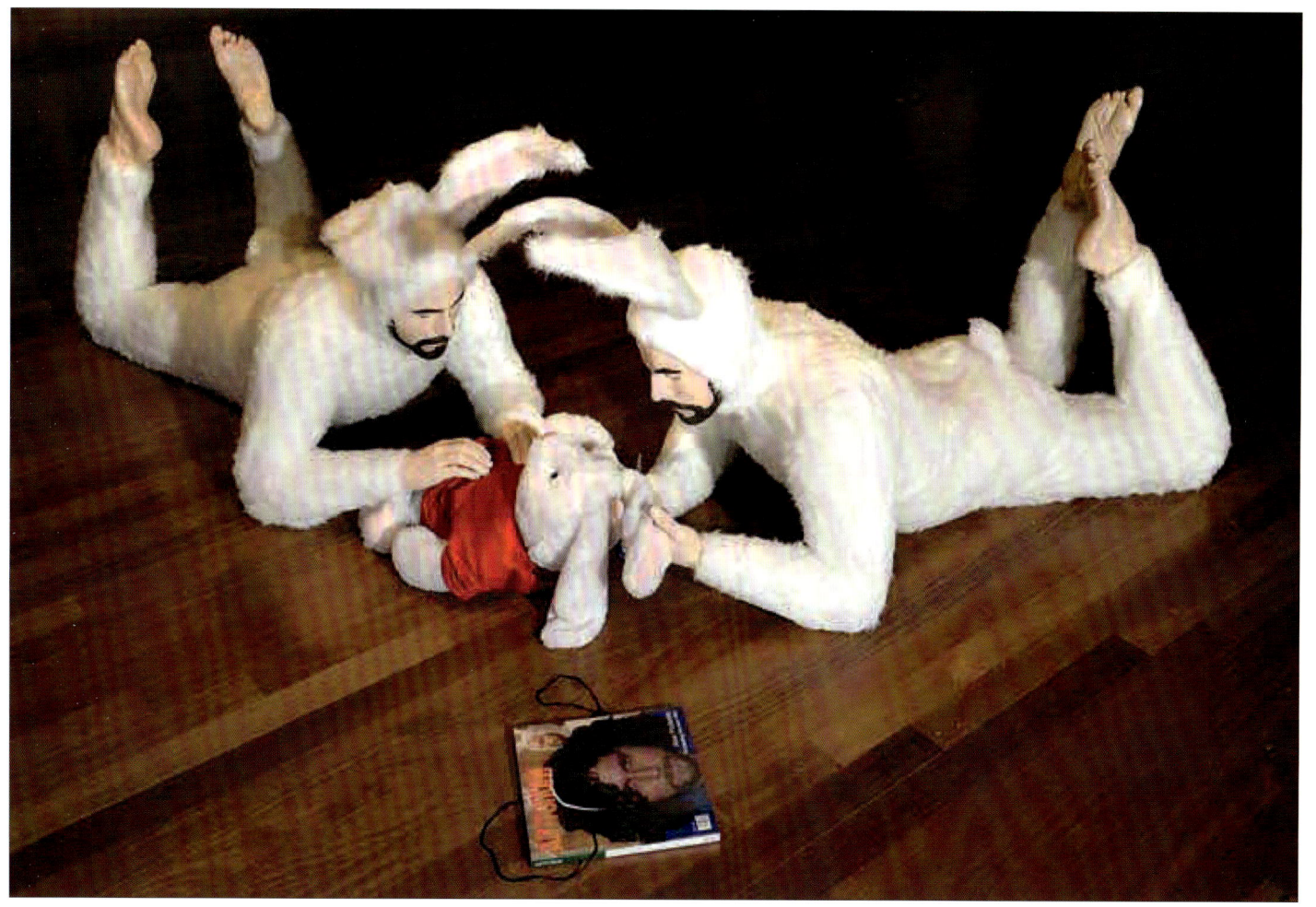

Self-Portrait as Bunnies (Hubris)   30" x 120" x 60"   acrylic fur, urethane resin, plaster, acrylic paint, fake Artforum

RAJKO RADOVANOVIC

Valjevo, Serbia, 1954

THERE ARE TIMES WHEN LITTLE IS TO BE achieved other than to allow the artist to speak for himself:

"I was born in a country that no longer exists. It is good to know one's own roots and where we come from, but I no longer believe that the concept of 'home' or that of 'belonging' can be dictated solely by the physical place of birth or by contemporary concepts of 'nationality.' The notion of self-identity is a spiritual choice rather than a political 'given'. After the collapse of the Berlin Wall, the disintegration of the Soviet Union, and the violent break-up of Yugoslavia, I used my work to explore the mechanisms of individual and collective traumas within transitional, post-socialist societies. This resulted in a series of work which explored people's moral standards and their requisite modification, which allowed universal acceptance of violence towards their fellow citizens. Both the acceptance from the countries who exported war and from those on whose soil that same war was staged. The statement in my work *A Precondition*, appears against a background of newspaper columns written in the Croatian language, referring to the fact that our modern political establishments, by influencing public opinion through the media, have promoted the notion of 'other' as a modern definition of 'enemy'. It is through this manufactured concept of 'difference' that moral justification is sought for inflicting violence towards fellow human beings. Living and working as an artist in different countries has confirmed for me that acts of oppression are not confined to military conflict and that the resultant trauma of such oppression is universal. To this day, art seems to me the only attempt to deconstruct the daily consent of bearable normalcy. Once one realizes the meaninglessness of one's own environment, the only remaining choice is to start to learn how to live with that fact. For me art has been and still is a clear modus of existence for an individual human being."

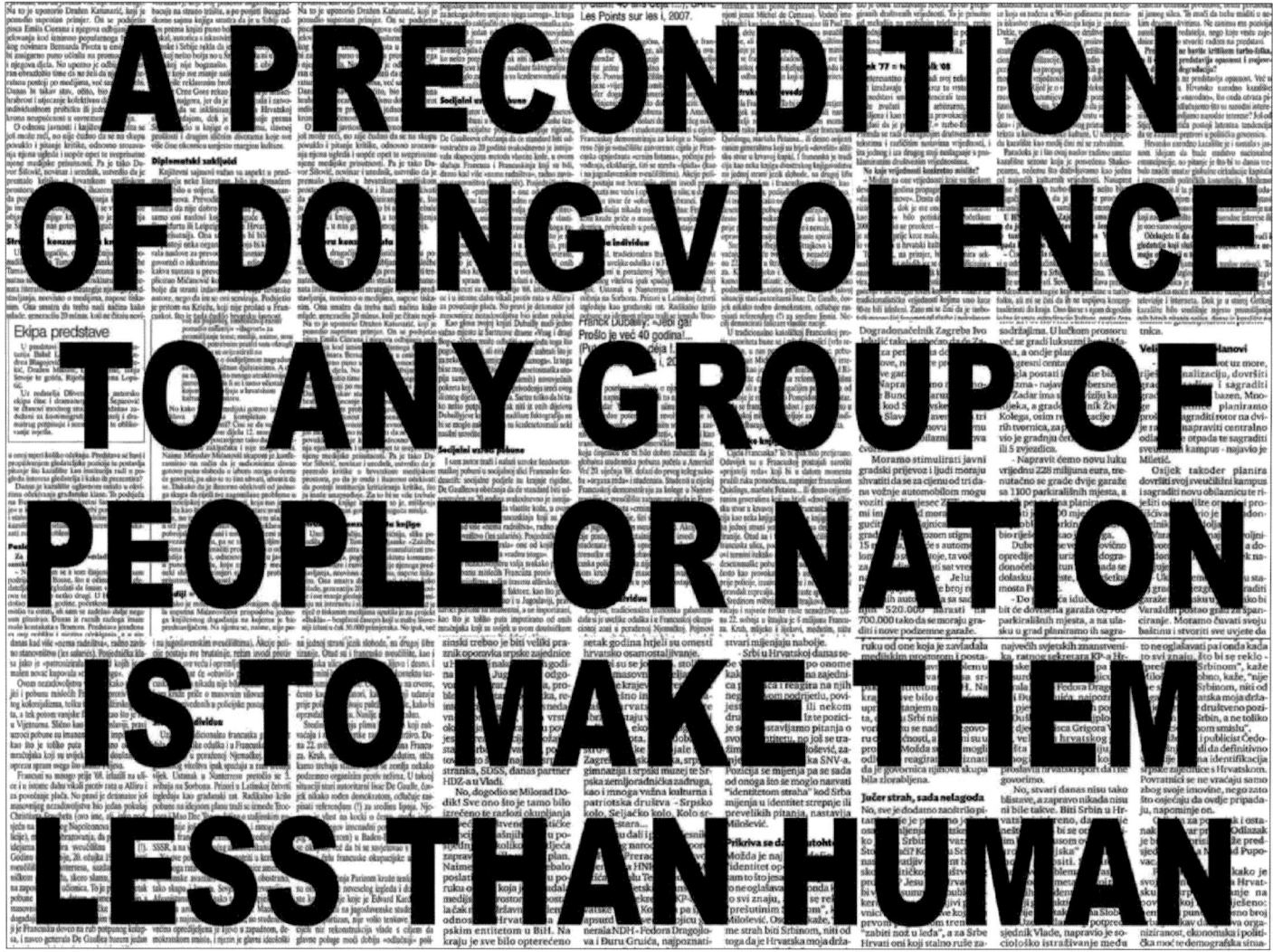

A Precondition   30" x 44"   silk screen print on stonehenge archive paper

REBECCA REBOUCHÉ

Franklin, Louisiana, 1982

who knows if the moon's
a balloon,coming out of a keen city

THUS BEGINS ONE OF E.E. CUMMINGS'S poems on the enchanted nature of this world we inhabit. Is it the moon or a balloon, or two cherries stitched to a cloud? Rebecca Rebouché's paintings inhabit this world with a child's picture-book inquiry, where effortless objects serve as metaphors for human emotions and ambitions. Tender, hopeful, and whimsical, these signposts are the reminders of a childhood not lost but maintained in the sustenance of human symbols, paintings which offer a panorama almost archetypal. Striped shorts, ice cream cones, toy sailboats. A white dress, butterflies and umbrellas. All anthropologic objects against peaceful, deeply-textured backgrounds of diffused grays, sepias and blues that manage to recall the fields in which Joan Miro's shape-games played. Though the humanity in Rebouché's canvases is evident, equally evident is the absence of human faces and figures. We are in a world of things that follow human consciousness as lovingly as *The Red Balloon* in Albert Lamorisse's film. Rebouché's technique involves a patchwork of fabric and paper laid on canvas and layered under paint. The layered elements projecting upwards through the image echo the quilting technique that is part of Rebouche's family tradition. She recalls what it was as a child to witness both her mother and grandmother assembling quilts from various fabrics. This tactile element, adding chafe to both background and primary objects, marries process to project and points towards the resiliency of craft reference in contemporary art. Rebouché's ultimate affect is lyrical and fanciful and gives whistle to a world where, to complete the e.e. cummings poem…

it's

Spring)and everyone's
in love and flowers pick themselves

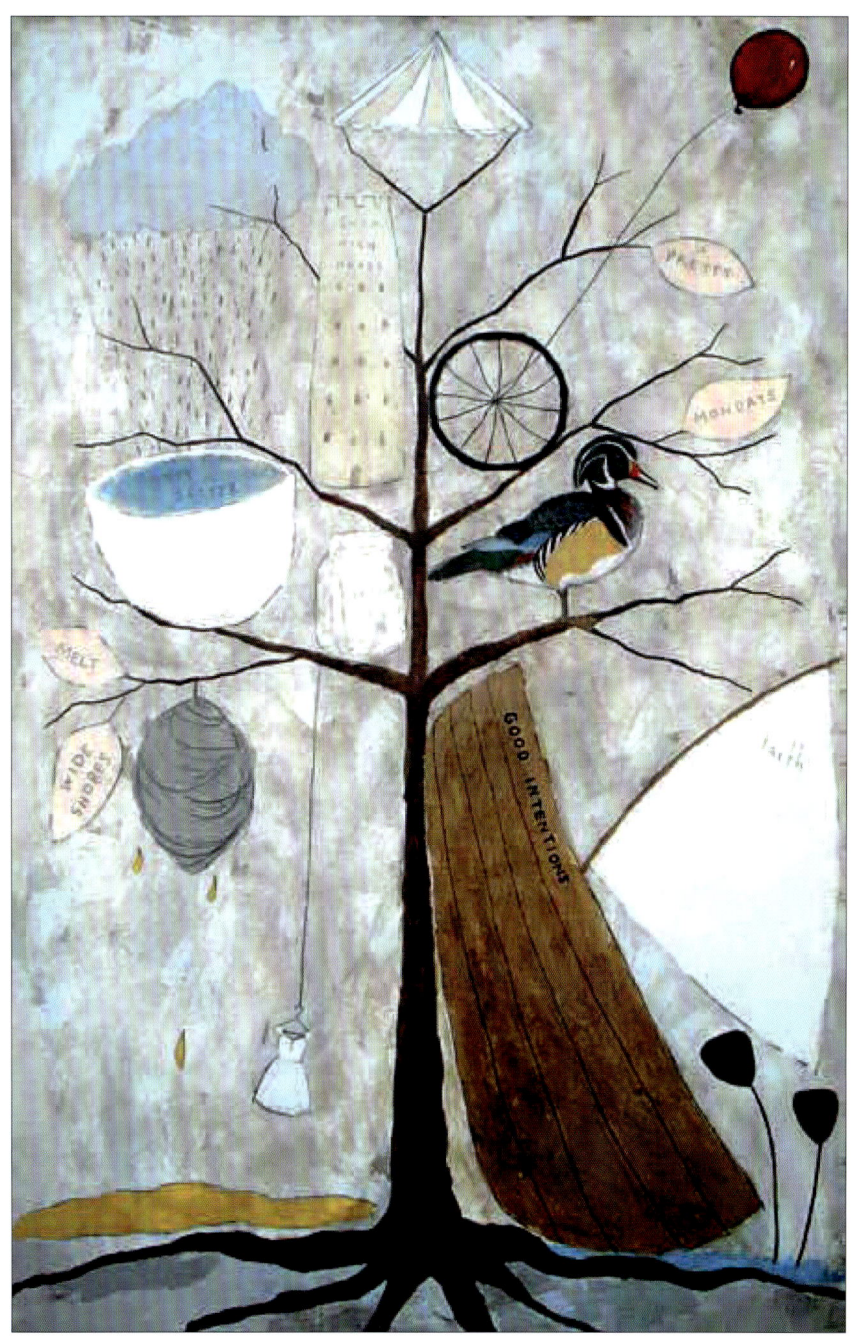

Honey Tree   72" x 48"   mixed media on canvas

AARON REICHERT

Owosso, Michigan, 1978

THE TEMPLES OF CELEBRITY ICONOGRAPHY mark our collective landscape. When the gloss of their unassailability breaks down, the skin curdles and the gaping holes of mortality become part of the visage. Aaron Reichert is a painter of mortality. There is nothing seductive in mortality; there is only tenderness. Reichert is interested in the American experience, the harsh roads of its history and consciousness as depicted by the faces of its icons. Reichert spent his formative years in (the aptly named) Hartland, a rural setting outside of Flint, Michigan. His father worked at the *i* while his mother taught English. This American heartland locale and a spirit of manifest destiny pervade in the choices of Reichert's subjects. Minimizing color to near extinction on a monotone background, Reichert paints Civil War generals, stars of Rockabilly, wrestlers, and Hollywood super-celebs. His figures are immediately recognizable; but while painters from Andy Warhol to Elizabeth Peyton affirm celebrity Pop status, Reichert's process is one of removal. Both *Grit, Clint Eastwood* and *Up Front, Jack Nicholson* take American toughs, pillars of Hollywood masculinity, and peel back their muscle. If their sexuality is not dislodged, it is now removed from the equation. Masculine beauty has been traded for another sort. Their image (status) remains no less large, but flayed; representation unravels into semi-abstraction with swirls of lines and fissures. These geometric forays, though, are not mere flourishes; they are the mortal details inscribed by time, the hardships of age; they are the immanent failures of flesh, the rotting human meat, the cracks in the veneer that no mortal can stave. There is no irony in Reichert's work. He is closer to the intent of Ivan Albright, who rotted away the beauty of Dorian Gray, than Gavin Turk, who immortalized Sid Vicious in a glass box. Painters who depict celebrity also create a critique of the cult of celebrity, and Reichert is not removed from that conversation. But it is not the conversation that fuels Reichert's work. While sustaining immortality in iconography, it is Reichert's technique of sympathy that restores the humanizing quality of mortality.

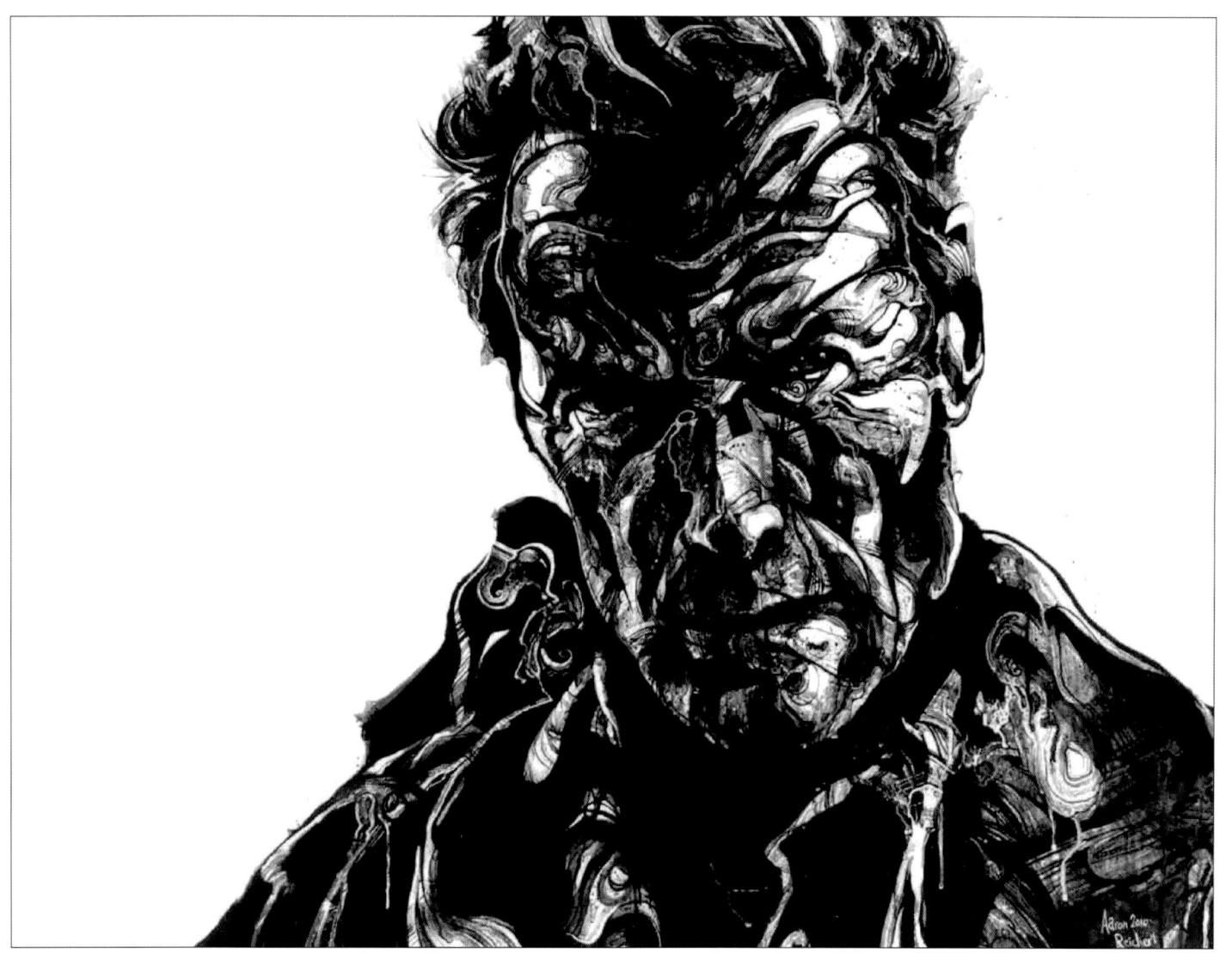

Grit, Clint Eastwood   40" x 30"   acrylic on canvas

TERRENCE SANDERS

Pineville, Louisiana, 1967

WHEN TERRENCE SANDERS WAS SIXTEEN–having been born in Louisiana and raised in Manhattan's Lower East Side, having suffered familial physical abuse, having run away from home to endure the harsh lessons of streets and rooftops, having learned to steal as well as survive drugs and sex and the excruciating uncertainty of his own existence–he met Jean-Michael Basquiat. This was in 1983, while the New York art scene raged in excess and Basquiat, the first black art superstar, tore graffiti from the streets and turned it into high art. Though by 1988 Basquiat would be dead from a drug overdose, his superstar status as well as his relentless work ethic, an outpouring of revolutionary canvases, and especially his self-aggrandizing transformation of lifestyle into a product, into art itself, is all part of Sanders's inheritance. Like Basquiat, and like Jasper Jones, and Henri Matisse before him, Sanders creates melancholic and electrifying images on canvases without center, where shapes, text, symbols, and portraiture balance into a conceptual harmony. Within his paintings one is as likely to find the iconic images of our current cultural personalities as a list of African-American heroes of time immemorial: musicians, writers, athletes, and leaders of social justice. These names are Sanders's influences and inheritance and therefore part of his art. Just as he is unhesitant to bring his own personal history into his work, so does his work reflect the culture which cast him. His painting, *Usual Suspects*, created in New Orleans during the eleven days Sanders remained in town during Hurricane Katrina, serves as a memorial to the victims of the attacks of 9-11-01. The list of names are of the victims, the images are of the atrocity's perpetrators; both are splattered with a violence of oil, appointing Big Oil's role in the tragedy. The fierce momentum contained within the canvas is set against an almost soothing yellow, which serves as a hue for the new day and new world that follows calamity. While much post-modern art deals with alienation versus meaning and prefers the conceptual over the concrete, Sanders contends to deal with solid issues of self, race, social identity, and the scams of our living days. In addition to painted canvases, Sanders works in photography, film, and video. He is the publisher of *Artvoices Magazine*, and created Jupiter Artprojects as a platform for emerging and mid-career New Orleans artists. He is also the curator of the Saratoga Collection.

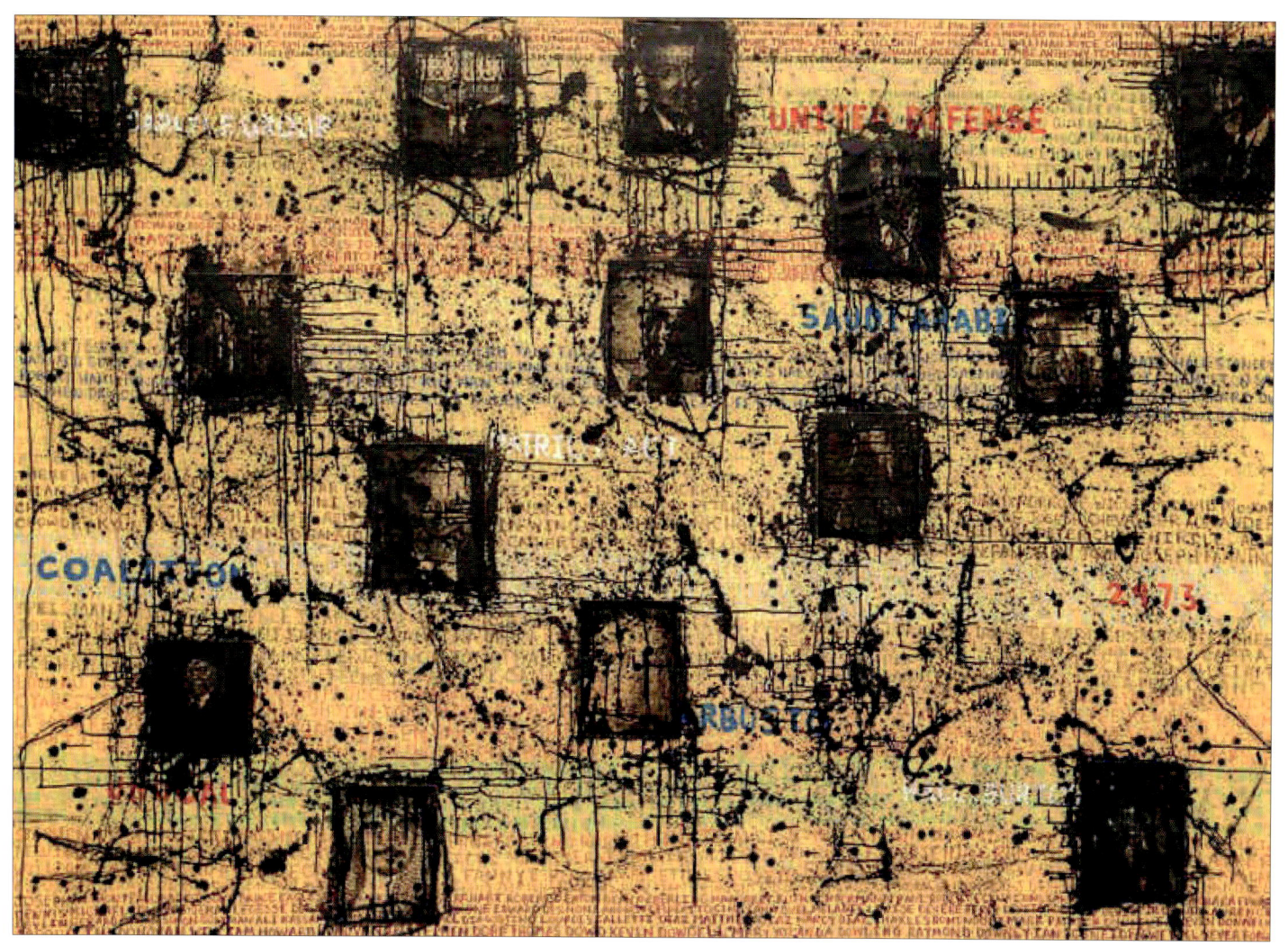

Usual Suspects   69" x 108"   mixed media on canvas

JIM SOHR

Waukesha, Wisconsin, 1954

FOR MORE THAN 40 YEARS, JIM SOHR HAS been painting distinctively zany images. His figures are more "human-eque" than markedly human. Strangely round or square heads, popping eyes, and long horizontal mouths are some of their characteristic traits. His nude women lounge languid, lazy, wide-hipped and big-busted, as if they'd slipped out of a Matisse and into a 1980s video game. Sohr acknowledges that he is most impressed with the paintings of Chagall, Picasso, Dali, and Walt Disney, and those influences show in his color scheme. The work is not subtle. Sharply defined lines and a firmness of foreground figure against geometric-patterned backgrounds are some of the defining qualities that have marked the long timeline of Sohr's work. Even the occasional soft pastel is contained within heavy dark borders. Sohr wants each individual item to stand up and stand out--to never be lost in minutiae of detail or background. Sohr's only formal training came from Angola, the Louisiana state penitentiary where he served half of a seven-year sentence for possession of a minimal amount of marijuana. During his incarceration he managed to get himself assigned to the art room, where he could work at any hour he wished with supplies furnished by the state. In 2008 his *Zor Bird*, a loony and child-friendly 15' steel, fiberglass, and aluminum sculpture was installed before the Children's Resource Library on Napoleon Avenue, funded though a public works initiative from the Arts Council of New Orleans with support from the Joan Mitchell Foundation. The full breadth of Sohr's career can be experienced within the walls of The Jim Sohr Museum of Modern Art, a two-story brick house located in the Katrina-devastated Chalmette neighborhood, which Sohr has turned into a studio and exhibition space for his vast and playful body of work.

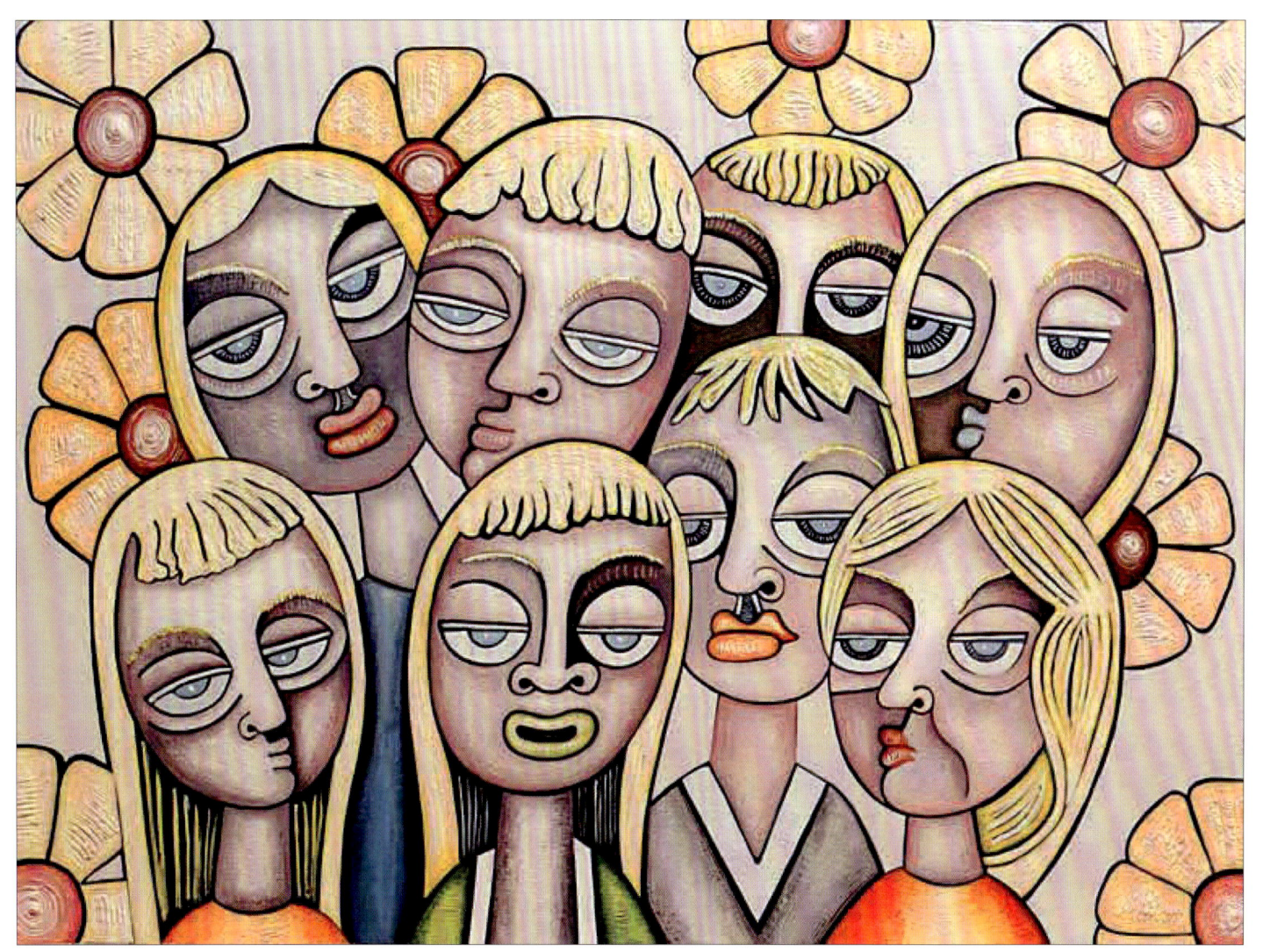

Blond Ambition   36" x 48"   acrylic on canvas

GENERIC ART SOLUTIONS (G.A.S.)

Matt Vis Quantico, Virginia 1965
Tony Campbell London, England, 1965

AT ANY NEW ORLEANS ART EVENT, FROM White Linen Night to Art for Art's Sake and certainly the upcoming Prospect.2, be on the lookout for the art performances by Generic Art Solutions (G.A.S.), the Gilbert and George style collaboration team of Matt Vis and Tony Campbell. The two impresarios have impersonated bronze statues, handed citations as Art Cops, and fashioned self-photographic recreations of Caravaggio's and da Vinci's *Last Supper*. Well-infused with humor while managing to draw parallels between historical and contemporary art, G.A.S. continuously makes conceptual forays with biting social commentary. Their exhibition at the New Orleans Museum of Modern Art, entitled *Déjà Vu All Over Again*, uses the British Petroleum Oil Spill as their artistic focus. G.A.S. has been a New Orleans based "two-man art team" since 2001, creating contemporary recreations of Classical works in video, photography, performance, sculpture, and painting. Campbell and Vis are founding members of Good Children Gallery, a collectively-run art space. With their fluorescent light sculpture, *OK*, G.A.S. asserts that all in New Orleans is now "okedoke." The two-letter dismissive, a quintessentially American idiom with a long history of use that includes once serving as an abbreviation for All Correct, the joke being that neither the O nor the K was correct, continues to pare down serious concern and calamity with a catch phrase not uncommon to political spin. If New Orleans is threatened with ecological disaster, drowning in back-room political shenanigans, oil-spattered by corporate abuse, its education system flayed, its streets pot-hole ridden, and its vital visual arts community threatened to be cut-off from government funding, G.A.S. would like to say, in the brightest of lights: *It's* OK.

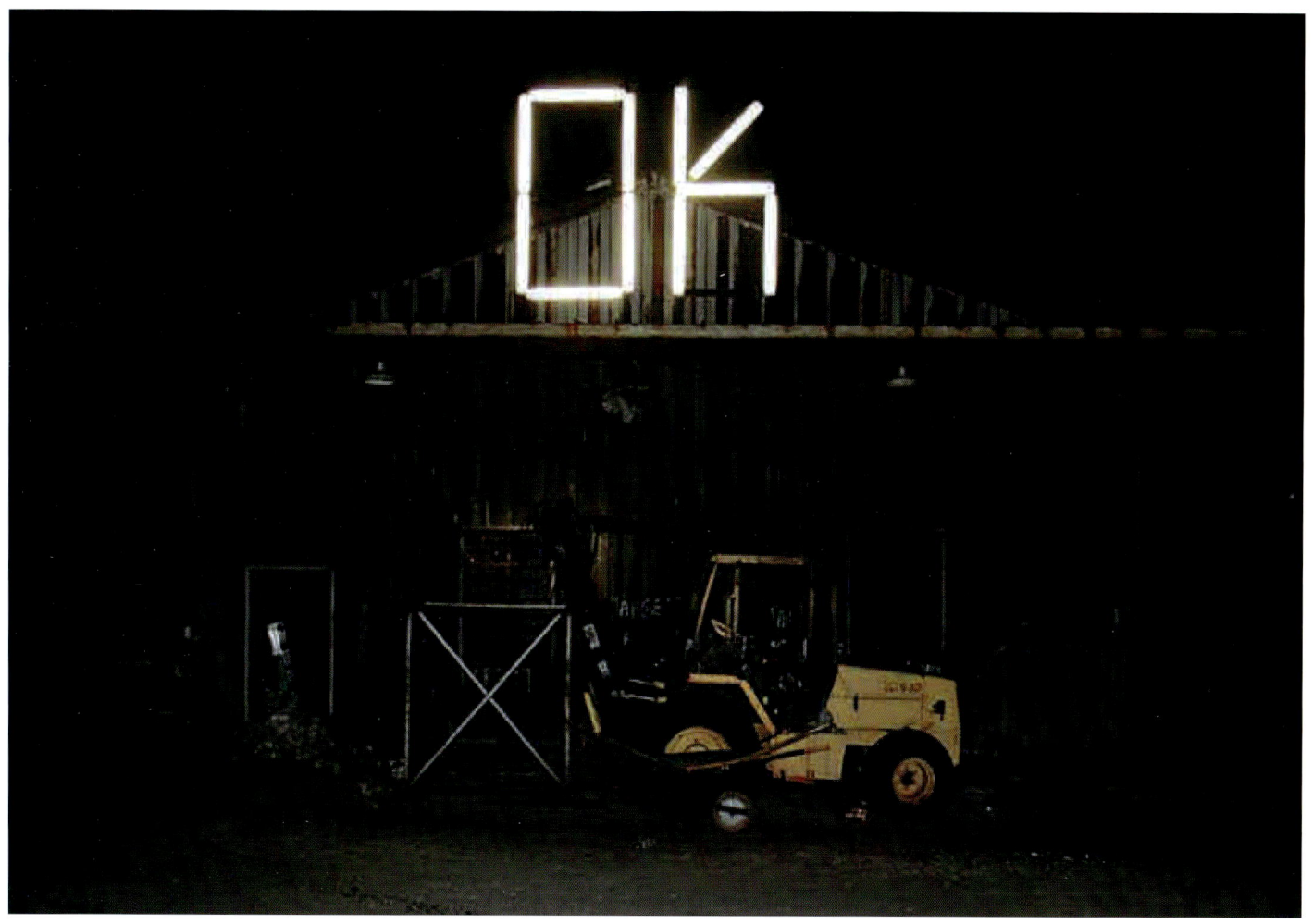

OK fluorescent light fixtures and wood

JAMESON STOKES

Alexandria, Louisiana, 1967

JAMESON STOKES SURFACED SOMETIME around the year 2003 after spending some time in Europe and Central America chasing his shadow. Before his departure in 1989 he began documenting the homeless on the streets of New York City. "I began shooting the disenfranchised and rejects of society. I am driven to the less fortunate because I am one of them and they are one of us," Stokes declares. Stokes rarely spent time in the darkroom making prints from his own negatives. He only supervised the making of his photographs with handwritten notes and instructions to the printing procedure at DuArt (NYC) and Professional Color Lab (New Orleans). Stokes continues to create provocative portraits of ordinary and not-so-ordinary citizens of the world with which we interact on a daily basis. "Everyone is relevant and we are all connected, no matter your religion, race, class or gender. I see beauty in what most consider ugly or unattractive. My photographs attempt to strip our layers of guilt, suffering, and self-hatred. I use photography to document and capture a fleeting and defining moment in life. I am the innocent or guilty bystander depending on the action of the moment. I connect with my subjects through the photographic process because it serves as a connective tissue to open a dialogue. Everyone deserves a chance to be heard, to be seen. The photographs preserve their statement of who, what, when, where and why. I am just the vessel that translates the human condition."

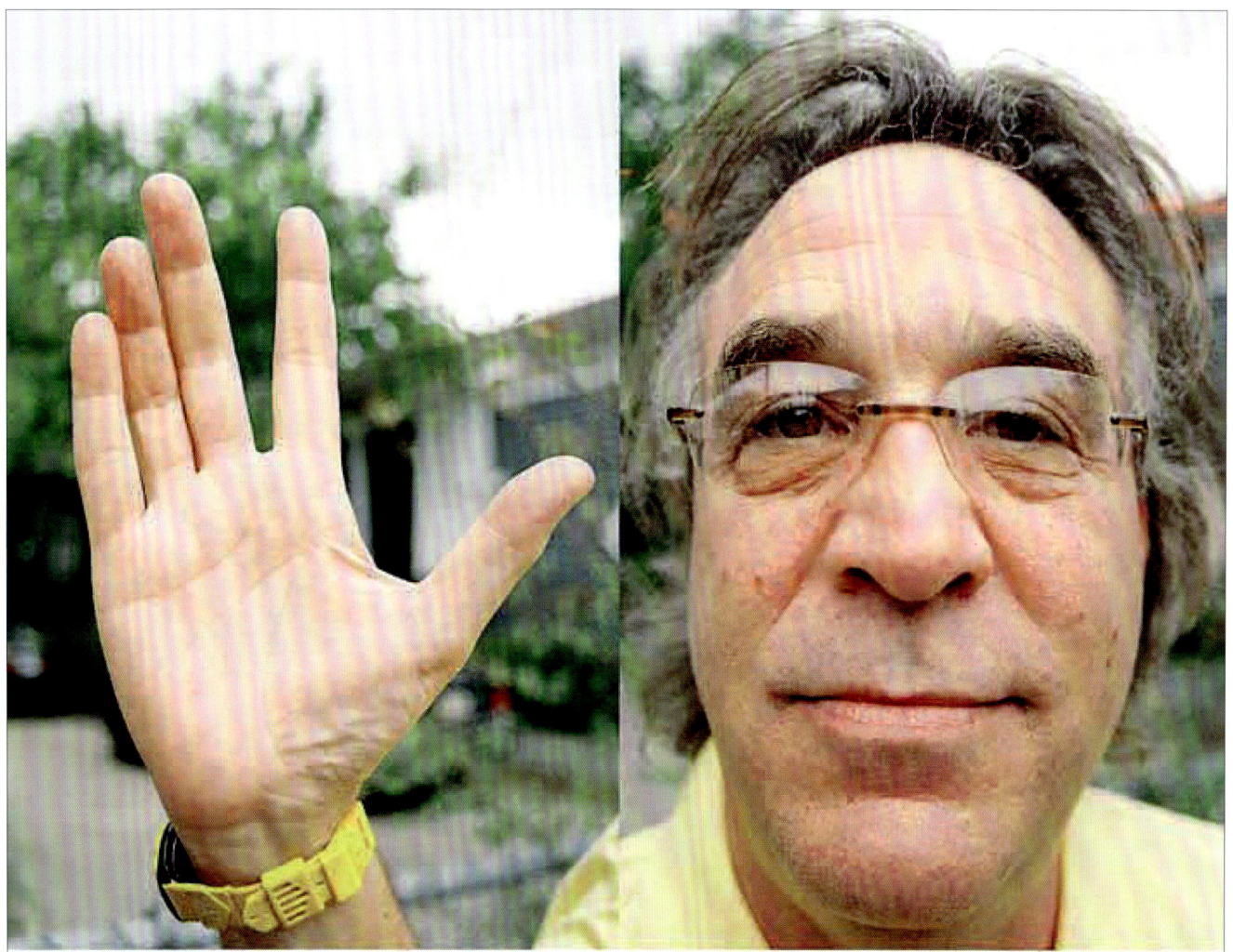

You are extremely intuitive and juggle many plans at once. You're organized and are constantly preparing for upcoming projects. You are pleasant and agreeable. You care about the feelings and needs of others.

People I Know   18" x 22"   digital color photograph

ROBERT TANNEN

Brooklyn, New York, 1937

ROBERT TANNEN IS INTERESTED IN STONES, in big boulders. He is interested in the planet, its composition, and the way humanity has fashioned itself to it, formed communities and living environments and engaged in a continuous process of scientific/architectural/sociological development. Robert Tannen is an artist who emerged from the New York City art scene of the 1950's and 60's to move to New Orleans in 1969 as part of the Gulf Coast rebuilding efforts after Hurricane Camille. His artwork incorporates stone, sheet metal, wood, paper, pretty much anything. Of his 50-year retrospective at the Ogden Museum of Southern Art, columnist Doug MacCash said that Tannen's art "is too aggressively intellectual, too defiantly unsellable, too oblivious of current fashion, and too just plain obtuse ever to have gained a wide following." However it sounds, the intention was complimentary, speaking of the magnitude of ideas behind Tannen's work. Robert Tannen is an engineer and urban planner. He is responsible for more than $2.5 billion in infrastructure development in Louisiana and Mississippi. He is one of the co-founders of the Contemporary Arts Center. Tannen's resume and work, which addresses community, environment, preservation, planning, process, and the transient nature of all things has made him one of New Orleans' landmark artists. His *Boulder #5* plays with ideas he launched when he transformed Lee Circle into a compass by placing a giant bounder at each magnetic point, marking them N, S, E, and W respectively. As Tannen explains, "New Orleans has no boulders nor large rocks except for those brought there to build jetties, streets and other urban structures. *Boulder #5* is one of a limited edition of named rocks not naturally found [here], and a reminder of Camille, a category #5 hurricane, the most serious, damaging and highest risk hurricane, more serious, damaging and higher risk than Katrina, and likely to happen some time in the future in this region"

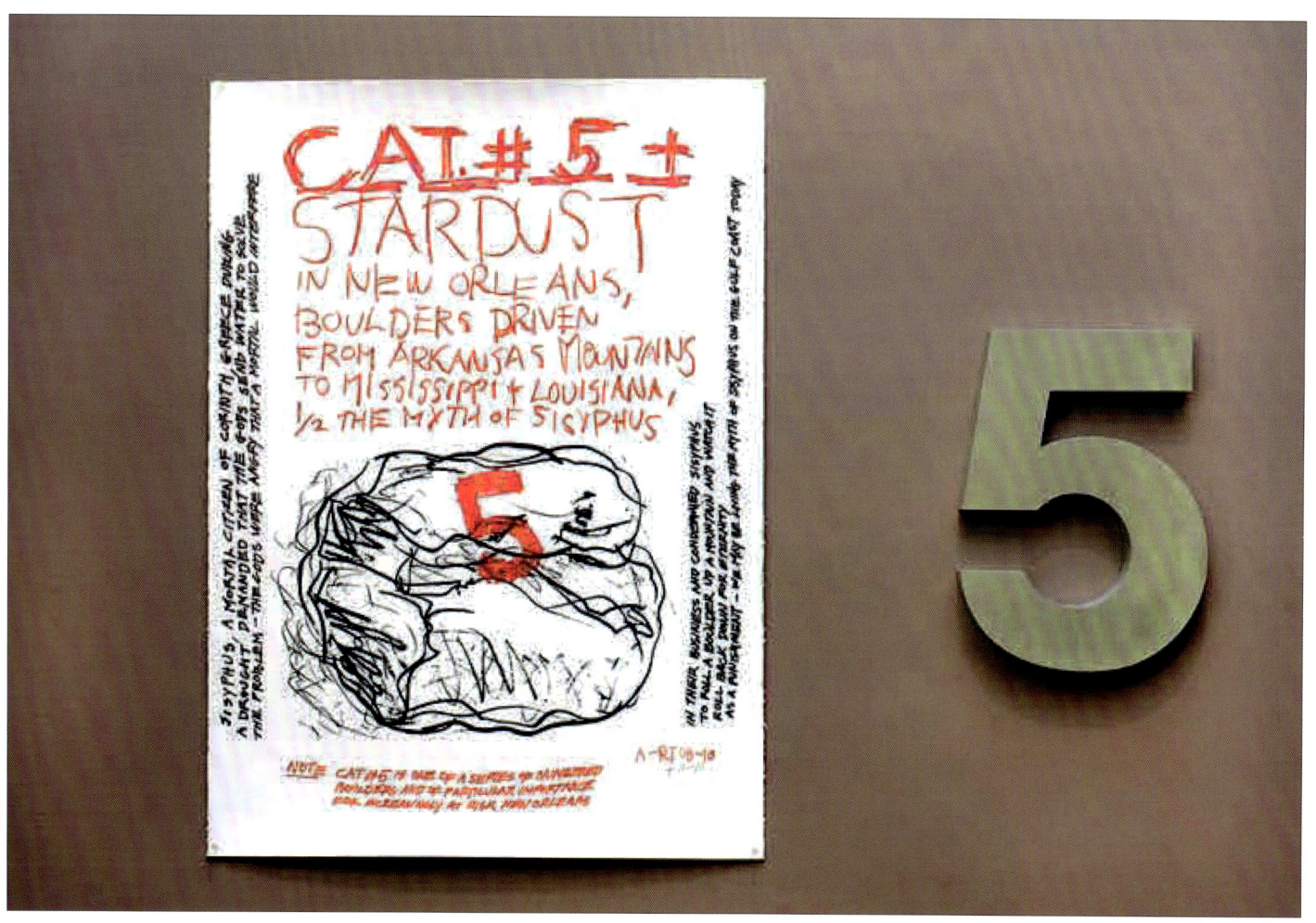

Boulder #5   72" in diameter   stainless steel and boulder

JONATHAN TRAVIESA

San Francisco, California, 1976

FOR TEN YEARS, JONATHAN TRAVIESA HAS been taking photographs of his broad circle of acquaintances in their personal settings. He centers them full figure and shoots them in black and white film outside their homes. The rest of the frame is devoted to the environment, their living spaces and the city of New Orleans which inevitably find their way into every shot in the form of: an abandoned player piano, wrought-iron gates, bicycles, stacks of salvaged wood, more musical instruments, chickens, many dogs, costumery, a carnival horse, discarded porcelain bathtubs. And foliage--lots of foliage. It is in the umbrage and undergrowth, in the creeping vines and fantastically huge frontage of the ever-blooming subtropical New Orleans environment, that the city makes itself known. For black-and-white photography, Traviesa's images are infused with a sense of green and a whiff of the fecund. The series is called *Portraits*. It has been published as a book by UNO Press and exhibited at the Ogden Museum of Southern Art as well as at the New Orleans artist collective The Front–of which Traviesa is a founding member. In the series, the marriage of portrait to environment is enhanced by the personal relations between Traviesa and his subjects. Traviesa assembles the cast. He meets them at their homes, where they are most at ease. The outdoor lighting keeps the illumination simple; no elaborate lighting kits or diffusing flags to intimidate the subject. Traviesa's camera is a simple Rolliflext twin-lens passed onto him from his father. The result is a pan-city documentation in the spirit of some of the great photographic surveys, such as Walker Evans and Dorthea Lange's Depression-era work for the Farm Security Administration. This is a New Orleans survey, though. The setting is sometimes rag-tag, but the spirit is high. Undisguised are the enthusiasm and *joie de vivre*, the pleasure Traviesa takes in his subjects and which his subjects take in their surroundings, their homes, their lifestyle and their city.

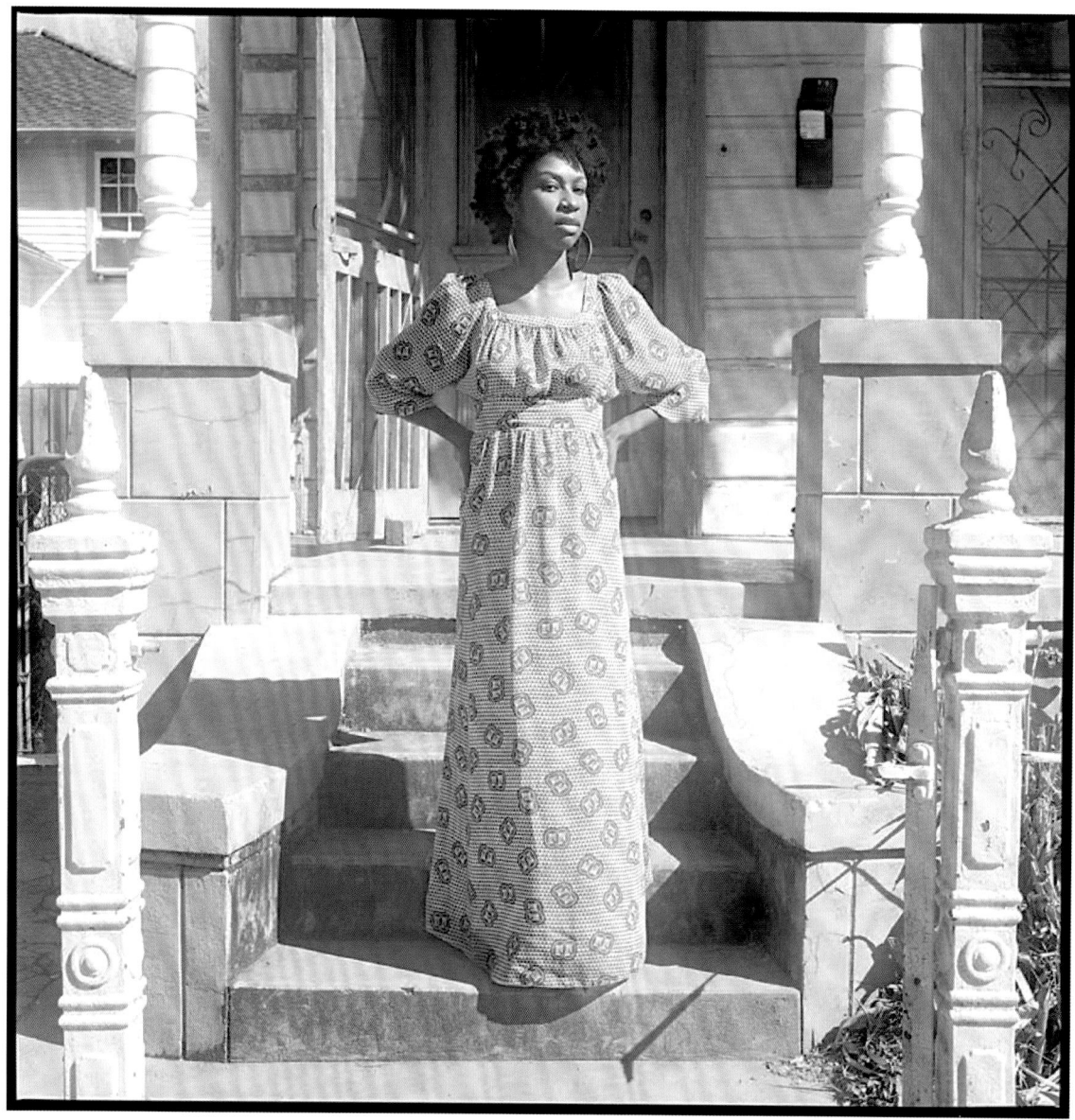

Portraits: Photographs in New Orleans 1998-2009   21" x 22"   b&w photograph

DAN TAGUE

Marrero, Louisiana, 1974

MULTIMEDIA ARTIST DAN TAGUE HAS MADE a small industry out of Money. No, not Money, which is a word almost as large as Economy. What Tague has made an industry out of is Currency, the intrinsically valueless commodity which comprises the physical aspect of our store of value. Tague subjects currency, specifically American bills, to an autopsy, eviscerating phrases, words, meanings, and ideas from its (material and aesthetic) legal tender. He plays origami games with the dollar bill, which, as Tague describes, is filled with "detailed decorative engravings, masterful portraits and architectural renderings, and elegant fonts," all which create the decorative allure Tague then folds and twists into collages of imagery and sometimes direct, accusatory language: "THE END IS NEAR," "STATE OF FEAR," "TRUST NO ONE," and "YES WE CAN" are just a few of the phrases Tague summons from currency, which he then turns into giclee on archival rag paper, convincingly close enough in texture and appearance to the bills in our pockets. Since these first forays, Tague has continued to make objects of power--tanks, planes, falling bombs, and soldiers--out of our currency. In *Destroyer* he stencils a battleship from the etched White House found on the back of a twenty-dollar bill. In *Good and Evil* he creates an actual tree adorned with grass, trunk, bifurcating branches, dangling cherries and dagger-shaped leaves made from dollar bills. Interesting that at the time of the Saratoga Collection, the sequel to the 1987 film *Wall Street* is being released, revisiting the era of the Me Generation, which epitomized admiration for greed, money, material things, and the drive to take them. Though his pillages into currency have given Tague's work a political bent, his essence is social commentary and street-conscious confrontation. There is something definitively self-referential in his forays into currency, a reminder that Art itself is one of the great swindles, one which involves the artist, critic, gallery owner, curator, and, most particularly, the collector: the one willing to authenticate the value appointed to a work of art by actually paying for it.

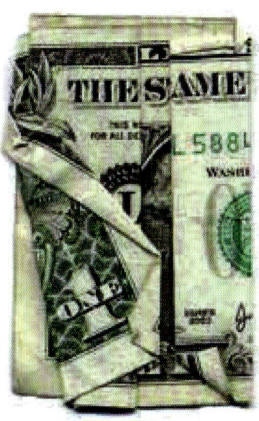 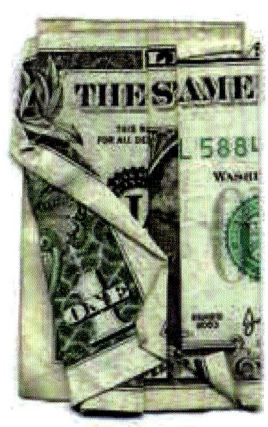 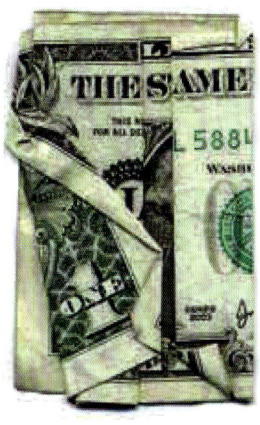 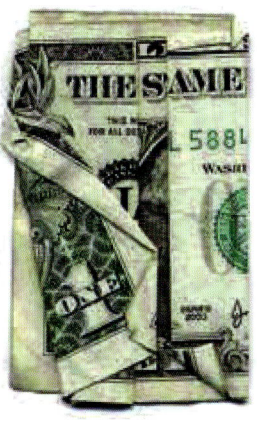

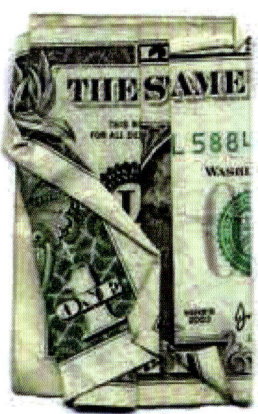 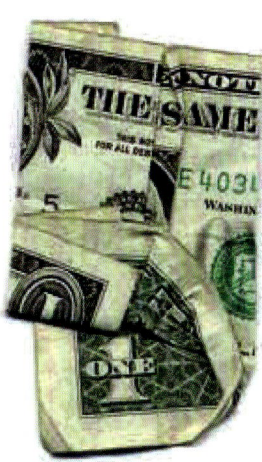 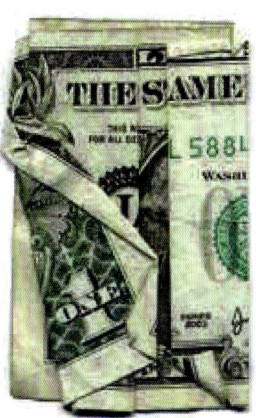 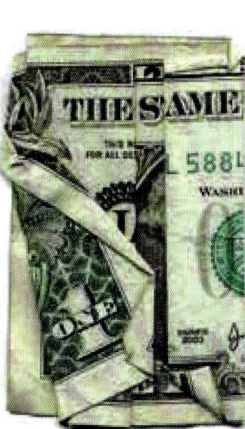

One of these is not like the others   36" x 60"   giclee on archival rag paper

PAIGE VALENTE

Fresno, California, 1978

WHILE TEXT SEEMS AN ANTITHESIS TO painting, an excursion into verbiage as opposed to the visual language the medium itself contends, a didactic dose of artists "working in text" since the 1990's seems almost to herald the social impact of the proliferation of email messages and phone-texts. Artists such as Sean Landers, Peter Davies, Christopher Wool, and Richard Prince all either supplement or rely exclusively on text to deliver their message. Paige Valente is likewise interested in text. Working in a large scale, Valente uses Gaffer's tape and acrylic on canvas or hard board to sprawl phrases such as "I WANT A REAL ONE" or longer meanderings about people drinking coffee, eating melon, and meeting in bars. The social is Valente's message, transferring the way we behave, speak, and desire to the visual. Always graffiti-like, Valente's affinity is for words as literal and typographic elements. Sometimes her sentences are laid out straight across canvas while others are caught in a whirl of high-energy activity, as if sentences were turning on themselves and each other. The playfulness and elusiveness of her text meanings is further infused with such titles as: *Addicktion Conviction*, *I Could Eat A Whole One: 923*, and *Goodie II: With His Beretta Right Inside Me, He Ain't Gon' Shoot*. Communication is Valente's concern, the means and intent of our outgoing messages and the manner in which our bevy of daily communiqués are received. Another branch of Valente's body of work is lush, mediumformat colored-pencil illustrations depicting human and animal personalities in everyday life. Standing among photographs, performing on stage, or negotiating urban streets, Valente sets out to make surreal synthesis of the personal and the animal in the collision of everyday settings.

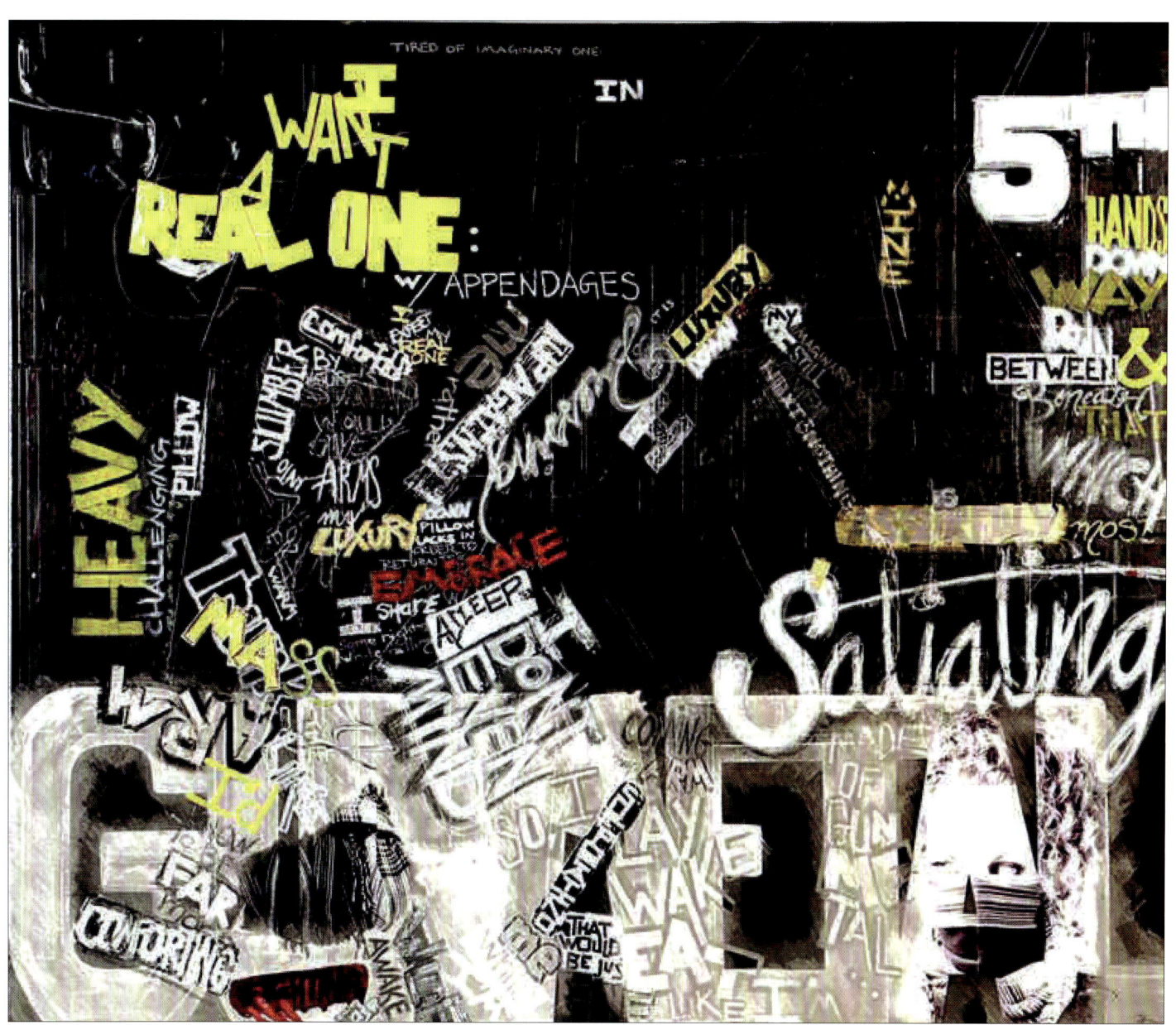

Goodie II: With His Beretta Right Inside Me, He Ain't Gon' Shoot
60" x 72"   gaffer's tape, artist's tape, acrylic, and mixed media on canvas

MIRIAM WATERMAN

San Fernando Valley, 1975

MIRIAM WATERMAN'S SERIES OF PHOTO-graphic self-portraits, *Verbal Abuse*, evolves from a relationship with a verbally abusive partner. The damages incurred, the strikes to her self-worth, as well as the self-personification of the abuses inflicted upon her, serve as catalysts of investigation. Waterman takes the words and accusations once thrown at her and prints them on her body using vintage rubber stamps inherited from her family's California agriculture business. She then photographs herself in black and white and inverts the image into a ghostly pallor, an X-ray of hot and cold contrasts. The words become more than tattoos, more than stamps; they are photographically ingrained, seared into flesh, assuming a physical property. Once the photographs are inverted, there is no re-touching, no manipulation. Physical blemishes become equally proprietary. Waterman is doing the opposite of what Cindy Sherman does when she adorns a costume and sets herself within a narrative. Instead of assuming a character, Waterman accepts the Self appointed to her by her abuser. The psychological portrayal is first self-absorbed then projected outward. Waterman also betrays the "show don't tell" lesson given to every first year creative writing, film, and drama student. Waterman immediately "tells" the dramatic content with a direct, printed accusation. The photographic inversion, besides incorporating process, allows Waterman to play with dualities. *I am this thing you say, but so am I more. This is my body, as well as its representation. Art is the thing which I do, and possibly what I am.* Like Tracy Emin, who addressed her childhood rape and embroidered the names of all her sexual partners inside a tent, inviting viewers to crawl inside, Waterman's direct incorporation of personal experience brings naked and chaffing intensity to her work.

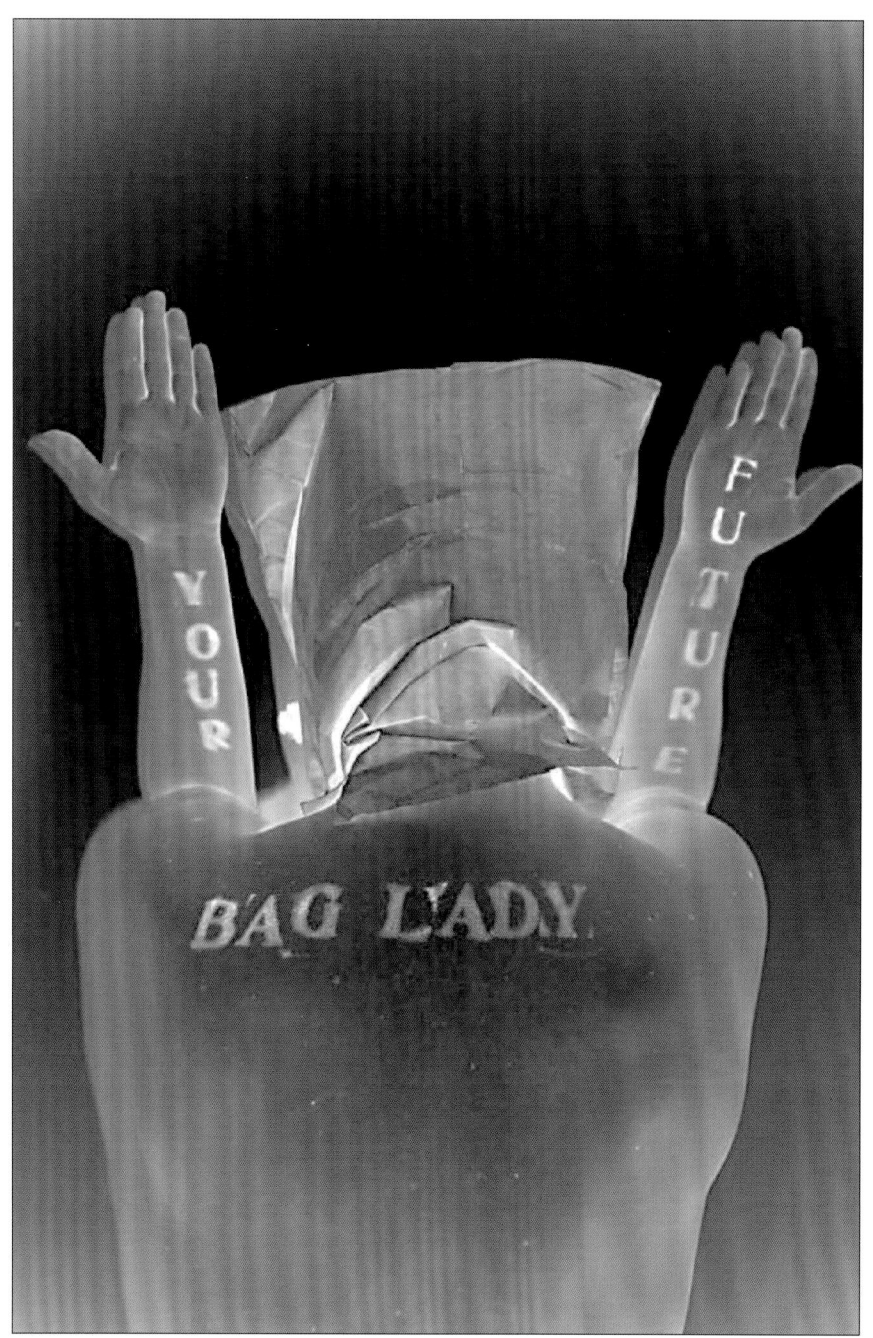

I See Your Future, Your Future Bag Lady   40" x 30"   b&w photograph

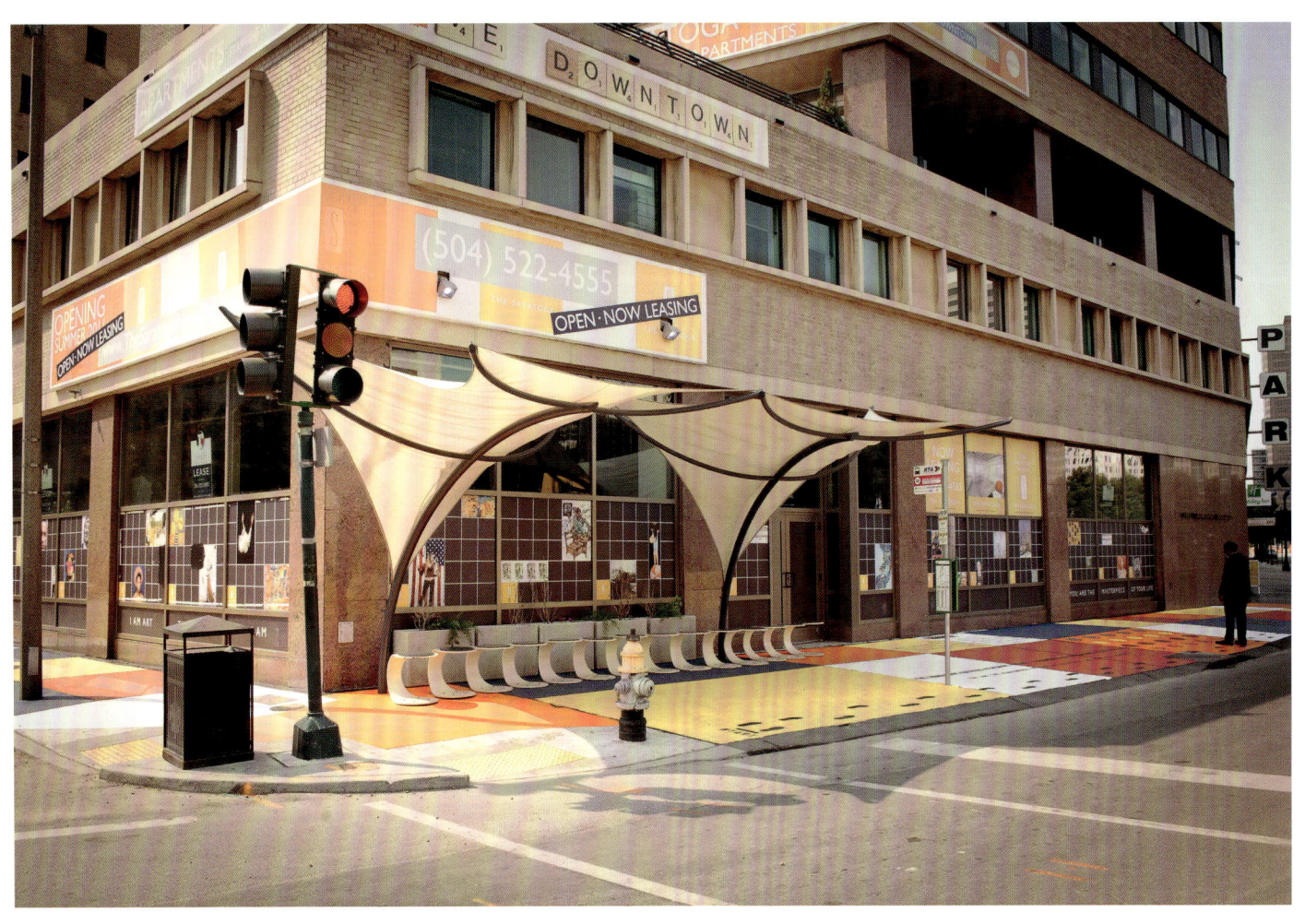

EMERGE

41 New Orleans' Artists from The Saratoga Collection
Curated by Terrence Sanders-Smith

In commemoration of the 20th anniversary of Hurricane Katrina's devastating impact on the city of New Orleans and, ultimately, the state of Louisiana, the Alexandria Museum of Art will be presenting the Saratoga Collection for exhibition. The storm claimed 1,833 lives, displaced families, wreaked havoc on the city's infrastructure, and represented a significant shift in the history of the United States. Since Katrina, the country and the world at large has witnessed a rise in "once in a lifetime" climate disasters from wildfires in Los Angeles to unprecedented flooding in North Carolina. While our country has seen its fair share of devastation in the last 20 years, it has also seen an explosion of creative output and potential.

The Saratoga Collection came to be in 2010 when developer and architect, Marcel Wisznia commissioned curator, Terrence Sanders-Smith to put together works by artists living and working in New Orleans in the aftermath of Hurricane Katrina. The resulting collection of works stands as a testament to the resilience of the creative spirit in the face of disaster. The storm may have physically damaged the city of New Orleans, but it did not dampen its artists' spirits. The artwork, music, poetry and literature that followed in its wake continues to inspire and move the public to this day.

The collection was first exhibited at the Ogden Museum of Southern Art before being permanently installed at the Saratoga Building in downtown New Orleans, from which it takes its name. It remained on display until 2020, when the building was sold to a large hotel chain. Terrence Sanders-Smith was then tasked with finding the collection a new home. Having roots in Alexandria, Louisiana, the curator reached out to the Alexandria Museum of Art in hopes of donating the collection in its entirety- a gift the museum's Collections Committee and Board of Managers enthusiastically accepted.

The donation of the Saratoga Collection was finalized in 2021 with plans to exhibit the collection in its entirety for the 20th anniversary of Hurricane Katrina. The collection, comprised of 62 works from 41 artists, brought a fresh set of artists, mediums, and topics to the museum's growing collection of contemporary art from Louisiana. Alongside the Saratoga Collection, Marcel Wisznia and Terrence Sanders-Smith also donated its sister collection, the Smith & Wisznia Collection, adding an additional 96 pieces in a variety of mediums to the museum's collection. Smith & Wisznia was exhibited in 2022, and the museum is thrilled to present the Saratoga Collection on exhibit from November of 2025 through February of 2026. We hope the works included in the show will inspire poignant conversations about Katrina and its lasting impact on the cultural and physical landscape of our state, as well as remind viewers of the importance of the arts in the process of healing and moving forward.

By Olivia Camayd Helmer Curator Alexandria Museum of Art

THIS MURAL IS DEDICATED TO THE
WE WILL FORGIVE BUT WE

Aaslestad, Wayne
Abaraca-Espinoza, Julio
Accardo, Paul
Acosta, Bertha
Acosta, Joanne E.
Adcock, John
Aiola Sr., Anthony
Alexander, Estrella
Alexander, Dale Cleveland
Alexander, Margaret L.
Alexie, Jr., Melvin
Alexis, Cecile
Alexis, Rupert Mylon
Alford, Hollis
Arceneaux, Louise
Alleyne, Joseph
Alleyne, Joseph
Allen, James, Jr.
Allen, Eddie L.
Allen, Charles Edward
Allen, James
Allen, John David
Allen, Kenrick
Allen, Lorraine
Allen, Susan
Allen, Sylvia Harriett DanielS
Alvarez, Louise Scie Raymond
Alverson, Rev. Donice Watson
Amiker, Maggie
Ancar, Evelyn
Anderson, Barney S.
Anderson, Tony
Andrews, Brenda
Andrews, Ferdinand
Anthony, Ruby
Arcement, Irma
Arceneaux, Betty
Arceneaux, Douglas
Archer, Gregory
Ares, Jose
Aris, Sophia Hasigianis
Arleth, Elsie
Armand, Garrett Michael
Armstrong, Lydia
Arnold, James
Ashbey, Rosemary
Ashley, Frank
Ashley, Lynnwood
Asmore, Edna
Atherton, Thomas Henry
Aubert, Edward Mccormack
Aubry, YvoNne Badon
August, Gertrude
August, Joseph
Augusta, Doris Fortner
Augustin, Leila Cook
Augustin, Theresa
Aultman, Sheila
Austin, Winona
Austin, Derricnicka
Austin, Derrick
Antoine, Bernard
Anderson, Keyiana
Anderson, Henry
Anderson, Carl
Alvis, Kevin
Allen, Willie
Allen, Leighton
Alfonso, Raechel
Alexander, Julie
Aguiler, Dr Clark
Adams, Kimerick
Adams, Jeremy
Accomando, Jamie
Anderson, Barney S.
Abdul Kareem, Majid
Alexander, Joneca
Adams, Ernest J.
ArcenEaux, Nanette
Allen, Lyda
Ash, Patricia Jeanne
Babin, Beverly
Babin, Jr., Justin
Babst, Delores Estrada
Bachemin, Sr., Mervin Joseph
Bacino, Frank
Bacon, Byron
Badeaux, Della
Badon Sr., Donald Ray
Bagley, Betty June Dehart
Betty Bagley
Baham, Christina
Baham, Warren
Baldwin, Norma Jean Bougere
Balthazar, Earl
Bane, Carl
Bane, Christina
Bane, Jr., Edgar
Bane, Sr., Edgar
Bangs, Tonia
Banks, Joseph
Banta, Lillian
Banting, Irene Weston
Barcellona, Walter
Barham, RichArd E.
Barkum-Taylor, Hazel Lee
Hazel Lee Barkum-Taylor
Barnes, Samuel
Barrett, Judith Marie Thomas
Barthe, Sr., Alvin Martin
Bastiansen, Bernt
Batieste Jr, Arthur
Batiste, Lawrence
Batiste, Shirley
Battenberg, Sharon
Baudouin Jr., Irby Telesphore
Baulden, Irene
Baumgartner, George
Baxter-Rothaermel, William
Bayard, Mildred Jambois
Bazley, Riscella
Beard, Ella
Beard, Sonia
Beason, Sr., Arzell
Beatty, Gladys
Bell, Kim E.
Bell, Stephano D.
Benigno, Gloria
Benigno, Lukey
Benjamin, Mary
Benjamin, Nercile
Benjamin, Sterling
Bennett, Carmen
Bennett, Edith
Berger, Harry
Bergeron, Uk
Bertucci Sr., Gerald L.
Best, Benjamin Hobdy
Betzer, Carol
Bieler, Norma
Bilich, Inez
Bingham, John
Bishop, Lando
Blackwell, Katherine
Blackwell, Malcom
Blanchard, Edward
Blanchard, Herbert
Blancher, Lawrence
Blancher, Marjorie
Blappert, Gloria
Blutcher, Nettie
Bohnet, Gloria
Bonono, Anna Mae
Bonono, Luke
Bonura, Rosemary Olivier
Boone, WilLie
Borges, Errol
Borne, Samuel
Bosarge, Sarah
Boss, Bulah
Bourgeois, Joe Lynn
Bournes, Rayfield
Bowen, Jamie L.
Bowes, Samuel Anthony
Bowie, Xavier
Bowser, Gloria
Boyd, Arthur
Boyd, Loretta
Boyle, Eugenie
Bradley, Dorothy
Brantley, Lee Esther
Braustein, Eugene
Breaux, Eunice
Breaux, Laura
Brecht, Marjorie M.
Bridges, Chris
Brill, Bernice Rae Schwartz
Brinston, Johnny
Brooks, Eleanor Mcdowell
Brooks-Anderson, Rosaline
Brossette, Joseph
Brouchard, Alma
BrOuwer, Mabel
Brown, Anna Mae
Brown, Clarence
Brown, Gerald
Brown, Laurence
Brown, Linda
Brown, Roosevelt
Brugger, Joseph
Brumfield, Mattie
Brumfield, Sr, Danny
Bryant, Clarence
Buckland, George
Buckner, Selina
Bumgartner, George
Buras, Lloyd
Burgess, Jannie
Burke, Mary
Burke, Thomas
Burns, Evelyn
Burns, Jerry
Burns, Winnie
Buse, Owen
Butler, Alex
Butler, Benny
Butler, Leroy
Butler-Bullock, Mary Ann
Buxton, Nick
Byrd, June
Byrd, Sydney
Byrd, Donna
ButLer, Arlene
Burris, Clyde
Burden, Freddie
Bullock, Alisha
Bryan, Clarence
Brunies, Craig
Brumfield, Veo
Brumfield, Avis
Brown, Ronald
Brown, Charlie
Broomfield, Kenyatta
Brooks, Warren
Brissette, James
Brim, Robin
Brignac, Charles
Bright, Albert
Bridges, Ebony
Breaux, Josephine
Bradley, Barren
Bowser, Julie
Bowers, Michael
Boone, Charles
Blanton, Suzie
Blanchard, Charlene
Black, Dr. Allen
Bingham, Joyce
Billa, Jose
Bernard, Donald
Bergeron, Dale
Bell, Eli
Battalio, Melissa
Batieste, Theodolius
Barrio, Stephaine
Barnes, Lillie
Barkins, Sabrina
Barbee, Richard
Babchin, Jefrey
Bernard, Derielle
Ball, Anna Rebecca
Baker, Elaine
Brackman, Louis
Brandt, Sr., Carl Vincent
Bulleman, Claire
Bonin, Daniel W.
Black, Hubert
Braganza, Maximiano
Bellanger, Jeffery J.
Benigno, Gloria
Benigno, Lukey
Blair, James
Babineaux, Darlean
Buxton, Deborah
Brenson, Curtis
Beaty, Jean
Brinston, Lemem
Browne, Peggy
Brown, Aivien
Barra, John
BRumfield, Danny
Baham, Warren
Bryant, Lashone
Brickley, Trechelle
Bitonti, Charles
Brannon, Anthony Hike
Beverly, Tillman
Becker, George
Blanchard, Loretta
Baochard, Alma
Bailey, Carolyne
Blais, Donald
Blanchard, Charlene
Bonhomme Simon, Patsy Louise
Breckenridge, Helen
Broussard, Dorothy
Brown, Raymond
Brumfield, Veo
Burden, Freddie
Burts, Henry Mitchell
Bryant, Jaquell
Butler, Bernie Jr.
Caimi, Billie
Caixeta, Benilda
Calhoun, Jr., Charlie
Caliste, Frank
Campieri, Joseph
CApetillo, Patsy Abella
Capetillo, Uk
Caple, Rachel Kentzel
Carpenter, Claude
Carson, Nathaniel
Carter, Lucy
Carvel, Rosa
Casby Jr., James
Casimire, Louise
Castle, Issac
Cerniglia, Sam Salvadore
Cevasco, Irma
Chaix, Gerald
Chambers, Frank
Charbonnet, Bruce
Charles, Donald
Cherrie, Onelia
Chester, Ricky
Chriss, Darryl
Christen, Jr., Charles Henry
Clauson, Victoria Collins
Clauson Iii, Yeager Andrew
Clements, Margarita R.
Clements, Irby
Clark, Shawnte
Clark, Roy
Claiborne, PhilLip
Christie, Jeanne
Cheshareck, Christopher
Cheeseman, Cheryl
Chauppetta, Charles
Charlene, Gerald
Charlas, Kelly
Chapman, Terry
Chan, Yan
Caruso, John
Carter, Lavarry
Carter, Eric
Carter, David
Carrie, Tonya
Carmouche, Kim
Carmouche, Cindy
Caples, Randall
Campbell, Frankie
Calhoun, Jerry Mark
Celestine, Mathilda
Corona, Mike
Corona, Anthony
Corona, Ricky
Collins, David
Chesnick, Richard
Cimino, Lawrence
Cunningham, Murray
Connie, Brown
Childress, David
ChildrEss, Robert David
Craig Jr., Lucius
Coldmen, Deshew
Calamusa, Barry Joeseph
Cheeseman, Cherylmarie
Cole, Frank
Crutchfield, Stephanie
Cavalier, Essie
Cecile, Alexis
Chambers, Ashley
Chapman, Joseph
Cheneau, Joan
Coleman, Lloyd
Coronan, Mary Claire
Cyres, Christable
Cyres, Clifton
Clifton, Warren
Coleman, Arnecker
Coleman, Darrel
Coleman, Johnnie
Coleman, Thomas
Collins, Ethel
Collins, Lylton
Comeaux, Evelyn
Comes, Guy
Common, Clarence
Conway, Patrick
Cook, Myrtle
Cooley, Wilmer
Copelin Jr., William Witz
William Copelin, Jr.
Cosse, Walter
Cotham, Donna
Cousins, Adele
Couvillion, Ned
Covington, Fetus
Cowsill, Barry
Cox, Frances Willie Lawson
Cox, Ronald
Creppel, Barbara
Cronan, George
Cronan, Mary
Crunk, Florence
Crutchfield, Wessie
Culpepper, Sam
Cummings, Norman
Cunningham Jr., Eli Russell
Cuquet, Nicholas
Cyres, Clifton
Cyres, Christable
Curtis, Matthew
Cummings, China
Craig, Donald
Cox, Calvin
County, John
Cornett, Clay
Corley, GEorgereina
Colman, Elaine
Collins, Shanika
Collins, Isaac
Collect, Sherrie
Collect, Mary
Collect, George
Collect, George
Coleman, John
Cochran, Shalisa
Celestine, Lawrence
Deceaseddanastasio, Micheal
Dabon, Stella
Dagnall, Joan
Dagnall, Ralph
Daigle, Doug
Nelson Daigle
Daigle, Irene
Dalier, Amelie
Damarin, Thomas A.
Dang, Kan Thi
D'arcangelo, Frank
Darsam, Mary
Daste, Rosalie Guidry
Davis, Calvin
Davis, Donise
Davis, George
Davis, John
Davis, Rosemary
Davis, TannEr
Davis-Jones, Deborah Hodges
Dawson, Elaine
Dawson, Leven
Day, Duffey
Deadman Jr., William Webster
Deamer, Ella
Deamer, Leslie
Dean, William Abbott
Dear, Herman
Deblanc, Elva
Decorte, Rose
Decour, Evangeline
Dedeaux, Uk
Dees, Clinton
Delafosse, Robert
Delatte, Zerelda
Delaune, Alan
Deluca, John
Denley, Jane
Dennis, Maggie
Depascual, Agnes
Desilvey, Donna K.
Desilvey, Linda Allen
Devine, Margaret
Dexter, Jr., Robert
Dickerson, Lawrence
Dickey, John
Dieck, MiltoN
Dimaio, Uk
Dimambro, Roger
Dinwiddie, Blanche
Doherty, Donald
Dorsey, Kerney
Dreher, Katie
Drury, Rita
Ducre, Margaret
Dugar, Ethel
Dugas, Edward
Duhon, Harrison
Duhon, Septeme
Dunn, John
Dunn, Thomas G.
Dupas, Harold
Dupor, Gladys
Dupuy, Pivon J.
Duvernay, Lorraine Rouzan
Duvic, Kim
Dyer, Mary
Durel, Chantel
Dupree, Lacy
Dubois, Kendria
Dubeau, Julian
Duarte, Guiomar
Divens, Gracie
Dimes, Matthew
Dillion, Dewayne
Decoteau, Thomas
Dear, Lillian
DawsoN, Grace
Davis, Moyhogene
Davis, Milton
Davis, Manwell
Davis, Junius
Davis, Anna
Darenburg, Ivory
Dansby, Louise
Daniels, Thomas
Daniels, Reanna
Dagle, Chevell
Dummet, Dr. Clifton O.
Dessommes, Mrs.
Davis, Taylor
Drez, Richard
Desrosiers, Marshall
Demetrakopoulous, Nike
Ditta, Billie
Davis, Jessie
Disodsdo, Penalver
Davis, Paul
Dragon, Leo
Dorsey, Christopher
Dannemann, Eunice
Darcangelo, Frank B.
Dixon, Mary
Dusuan, Virginia
Dorris, William
Doe, Jane
Doe, Jane
Doe, Jane
Doe, Jane
Doe, Jane
Doe, Jane
Doe, Jane
Doe, Jane
Doe, Jane
Doe, Jane
Doe, John
Doe, John
Doe, John
Doe, John
Doe, John
Doe, John
Doe, John
Doe, John
Doe, John
Doe, John
Doe, John/Jane
Doe, John/Jane
Doe, John/Jane
Doe, John/Jane
Doe, John/Jane
Doe, John/Jane
Doe, John/Jane
Doe, John/Jane
Doe, John/Jane
Doe, John/Jane
Doe, John/Jane
Doe, John/Jane
Doe, John/Jane
Doe, John/Jane
Eaton, Patsy Mitchell
Ebanks, Kemron
Edwards, Harry
Edwards, Joseph
Edwards, Lorraine
Edwards, Marjorie
Eiserloh, John
Eleby, Clementine
Ellis, Amella
Embry, Russell
Emerson, Joan
England, Robert
Estarlich, Michael
Ester, Edward
Ester, Feado
Estes, Gregory
Eustis, Charlotte
Evans, Daniel
Evans, Norman
Evans, Jr., Louis
Everett, Emmett
Everidge, Ronald
Ewale, Tesfalidet
Ewing, Thelma Wilkinson
Expose, Troy
Eugene, Reginald
Eugene, Ramona
Estervan, Sylvia
Edwards, Morris
Edwards, Ishandra
Edgecomb, Elizabeth
Ebbitt, Melanie
Easterline, Marvin
Emerson, Joan Hupp
Evans, Hubert
Elmansura, Sulemann
Ewing, Micheal
Espadrum, Daphyne
Estel, Clemons
Evans, Louis, Jr.
Edmondson, William
Eastern, James
Eaton, Viola
Fahrenholtz, Helen
Falcon, Larry
Falcone, Michael
Falcone, Tony
Falley, George
Falley, Shirley
Farzande, Ervin
Farzande, John
Fazande, Alvin
Fazande, Bernadette
Ferguson, Shelly
Ferrara, Carrie
Fisher, Deborah
Flemming, Clarence
Flint, Prosper
Ford, Alma
Ford, Lottie
Forrest, Hubert
Foster, Lynette
Francis, Ella
Francois, Benjamin
Franklin, AnnaIlese
Franklin, Charles
Frazier, Pearl
Frazier, Ruby
Freeman, Ethel
Fridley, Doris Evelyn Baer
Friedman, Angel M.
Frischertz, Maxine
Frymire, Connie L.
Fuhrmann, Caroline
Fuller, Warren L.
Funk, Robert
Funches, Johnathon
French, Stacy
Freeman, Lionel
Freeman, Allen
Francois, Tami
Francois, Marie
Fontaintte, Brenda
Flowers, Juan
Flores, Jose
Flemings, Laquincia
Fisher, Cynthia
Fields, Robert
Felder, Onell
Ferdinand, Brandon
Foxers, John
Feeley, Larry
FiliPik, Patrick
Fakes, Wilema
Fontanna, Melanie
Fassit, Crystal
Felix, Patrica
Francis, Sidney
French, Stacy
Gagliano, Charles
Gagliano, Shirley
Gaillourd, Wallace
Galatas, Jr., Arthur
Galler, Eva
Gallodoro, Tufanio
Galloway, Jerry
Garcia, Eugene
Garcia, Zermeno
Garcia-Pineda, Gerson
Gardener, Mario
Garrison, Marguerite
Gartman, Maxine Alfonso
Gastinell, Ellery
Gauthier, Ruby
Gayle, Shirley
Gibson, Robert
Gifford, Edward
Gifford, Nadine
Gill Iii, Joseph
Gilmore, ErnesT
Ginart, Father Arthur
Giuffre, Vincent
Godbold, Gerald
Godfrey, Delores
Godwin, Catherine
Godwin, Thelma
Goff, Danny
Goffner, Preston
Gomez-Hernandez, Adolpho
Gonzalez, Donna
Gonzalez, Dulce Marie
Gonzalez, Maria Del Los Angeles
Gonzalez, Rosa
Gordon, Mary
Gourgues, Mary
Gourrier, Alfred
Grant, Marcus
Greathouse, David
Green, Joyce
Green, Marion
Green, Rita
Green, Shanai
Gregg, William
Griffith, Lorraine
Grimes, Ayrie
Grover, Bessie
Grunik, George
Gryco, Faye Roberie
Gueydan, John
Guillory, Robert
Gulotta, Charles
Gulotta, Dorothy
Gumnick, Elfreida
Gunnells, Beverly
Gurtner, Ura
Guitroz, Cyril
Guilbeau, Selena
Guilbeau, Christopher
Griley, Anthony
Gregory, Ronnie
Green, Donald
Gray, Michael
Gray, Kayla
Graps, Ernest
Gore, William
Gloster, Darren
Ginart, Arthur
Gilmore, Kevin
Gills, Byron
Genins, Chuck
Gatewood, Todd
Gandolfi, Cheryl
Gallagher, Thomas
Galindo, Stephanie
George, Margaret
Green, Janice
Gifford, Reginald J.
Gifford, Jr., Elmer J.
Gaubert, Sr., Lloyd F.
Gills, Byron
Goss, Martha
Gary, Thomas
Gales, Hugh
Grush, Ruth
Gabriel, Eldridge
Graving, Kyle
Gochez, Jose
Gen.Thokozani, Tsvangirai
Guidry, Hazel
Gross, Matthew H
Gilmore, Lynett
Green, Corey
Griffin, Geoffery
Gauger, Wendy Sue
Griffiths, John C.
Guiffre, Vincent
Hackett, Gertrude
Hackett, Leona
Hains, Gilda
Hall, Azemo
Hall, Carrie
Hall, Raymond
Hamilton, Mary
Hansen, Mary
Hardeman, Iris
Harold, Rosa
Harris, Christopher
Harris, Pearl
Harris, Rachel
Harris, Rudolph
Harris, Virginia Rita
Harris, Booker
Hart, Martha
Hartdegend, Shirley
Harvey, Oliver
Haspel, Robert
Hawkins, Mary
Hawthorne, Mary Kirby Lea
Haynes, Paul
Haywood, Mattie
Hebert, Isabelle
Hebert, Wilbur
Hein, Rosie
Henry, Edmond
Henry, Gladys
Henry, Janice
Henry, Thomas
Herbert, Ethel
Hernandez, Audrey
Herndon, Rosemary
Heyl, Norris
Hicks, Ronald
Hilber, Chieko
Hilborn, Jules
Hill, Jim
Hillard, Marie A. Burbridge
Hilliard, Kevin
Hingle, Celeste
Hingle, Dorothy
Hinkel, Audrey
Holland, Dorothy
Holley, John
Holloman, Dorothy
Holloway, Delia
Holmes, Vincent
Holton, Alma
Horn, Clarise
Hose, Amelia
Hotard, Bonitacia
Howard, Lethea
Howard, Roberta
Howley, John
Hoyt, Mary Louise Fleming
Huard, George
Hubbard, Raymond
Hulbert-Manning, Faith Marie
Humphrey, Adella
Humphrey, Daisy
Humphrey, Lloyd
Hunafa, Al-Amin
Hunter, Della
Hurley, Odessa
Husband, Herman
Husley, Alonzo
Hutcherson, Jr., George
Hutzler, Alice
Hyatt, Jean
Hyatt, Arthur William
Hymel, Daryl
Hymel, Edgar
Hyre, James
Hyre, Shamsi
Hutchinson, Gregory
Huskin, Ruby
Hunter, Logan
Hunter, Latonya
Hulbert, Celven
Hughes, Huey
Hudson, Melvin
Howard, Gary
Hovanac, Andrew
House, Judy
Holmes, Jerry
Hollings, Debra
Ho, Thao
Hills, Courtney
Hicks, Darnel
Hicks, Darnel
Hester, Allysha
Herrera, Benito
Henry, Nadai
Henry, Granbille
Hendry, Kate
Hendry, Bob
Helms, Lakisha
HAynes, Latise
Haynes, Georgia
Hawkins, Neal
Harvey, Jesse
Harris, Rebecca
Harris, Patricia
Harris, Kerin
Harris, Katie
Harris, Booker
Hardin, Cathy
Hancock, Rebecca
Hampton, Lofette
Hammond, Stephanie
Hamilton, Charese
Hall, Trinity
Hall, Deborah
Hall, Cheryl
Hall, Celeste
Hagger, Ivory
Hackett, George
Hyer, Ralph V.
Herman, Avram Charles
Hoffman Jr., George
Hazel, Ian
Hicks, Cassandra
Hailey, Lynette
Halleland, Gary
Holley, John
Hooks, Rebbeca
Holzner, CarloS Alfredo
Harkins, Martha
Herman, Bernard
Hitt, Kenneth
Houghton, Mark
Hunter, Theadore
Hinkel, Audrey
Hopkins, Sr., Arvah Mansell
Huynh, Tan
Hershberger, David
Hebert, Kenneth
Hubbard, Earl
Harper, Danielle
Hamilton, Ortegas
Harris, Alex
Helbron, J.
Holmes, Kathryn
Houston, Gene
Hughes, Huey
Jachim, Robert
Jacko, Karnettia
Jackson, Alcede
Jackson, Antonia
Jackson, Eddie
Jackson, Elizabeth
Jackson, Emelda
Jackson, Ernestine
Jackson, Gladys
Jackson, James
Jackson, MyrtlE
Jackson, Rocksey
Jackson, Rosa
Jackson, Royal
Jackson, Russell
Jackson Sr, James
Jackson-Daly, Nora
Jacques, Dorothy
James, Gertie
James, Keith
James, Michael
James, Geneva
James, Sr., Arthur
Jamison, Jr., James
Jefferson, Aleria
Jenkins, Georgia
Jenkins, Joseph
Jenkins, Thomas
Johns, Delores
Johns, Lydia
Johnson, Althea
Johnson, Gerald
Johnson, Geraldine
Johnson, James
Johnson, John
Johnson, Mabel
Johnson, Mary
Johnson, Preston
Johnson, Willie
Johnston, AnthoNy
Jolly, Thomas
Jones, Infant Male
Jones, Anthony
Jones, Ella
Jones, George
Jones, J.B.
Jones, Sr., Cornelius
Jordan, Vicki
Joseph, Mayola
Joseph, Ruby
Justin, Roscoe Richar
Joseph, Johnnie
Jones, Herman
Jones, Dawayne
Jones, Crystelle
Jones, Clinton
Jones, Charles
Jones, Anie
Johnston, Chanell
Johnston, Bridgett
Johnson, Wilfred
Johnson, Veronica
Johnson, Ricquille
Johnson, James
Johnson, Darrell
Johnson, Clifton
Johnson, Bobby
Jimenez, Benny
Jenkins, RoberT
Jefferson, Lawrence
Jefferson, Aaron
Jeanmarie, Quilton
Jarboe, Harold
James, Henry
James, Benny
Jackson, Stephond
Jackson, Latonya
Jackson, Kentrelle
Jackson, Jesse
Jackson, Betty
Jackson, Azaline B.
Johnson, Keith A.
Jackson, Bobby
Juneau, Ruth
Johnson, Helen
James, Benny
Jhonson, Charles
James (J.C.), Walker
Johnson, Thelma
Jones, Heresa
Jackson, Elain
Jackson, Mitchell
Jackson, Monroe
James, Virginia Aitke
Jarrell, Felder
Jeanmarie, Quilton
Johnson, IrviNg
Johnson, Samuel
Johnson, Wesley
Johnson, Wilfred
Jones, Crystal
Jones, Fred John
Jones, Gerald
Jones, Lloyd
Jordan, Helen Grace
Joseph Jr., Frank
Joseph, Junius
Labanca, Carmen
Labasse, Daniel
Labat, Mary
Lacarbiere, John
Lachney, Clifton
Lachney, Jeffrey
Lacoste, Althea
Laddin, Ronald
Lafayette, James
Lafrere, Nina
Lagasse, Merle
Lainez, Albertine
Lala, Althea Martin
Lala, George M.
Landry, Carla
Landry, Neomi
Landry, Iziel
Landry, Muronda
Landry-Prevost, Lilith
Lang, Helen
Lang, Nelson
Larive, Lurnice
Larive, Leroy
Larmeu, Elvera
Larre, Helen
Lastie, Cynthia
Latino, Marie
Lattanzi, William
Laudumiey, Mathilde
Lauga, Uk
Laughlin, Helen

VICTIMS OF HURRICANE KATRINA.
WILL NEVER FORGET.

aughlin, H. Sue
aur, John
aw, Debra
awrence, Wesley
awrence, Willie
e Boef, Louis
eblanc, Gladys
ebourgeois, Julia
ee, Austin
ee, Simon
ee, Thomas
efler, Betty
eslie, Austin
evasseur, Carl
ewis, Doneika
ewis, Nicole
ewis, Patricia
ewis, Rickie
ind, Mary
iuZza, Dominique
ong, James
onon, Mary
opez, Frank
opez, Todd
ott, Shirley
ouper, Edmund
ouros, Harry
ove, Sr., Herbie
overde, Vivian Clare
owry, George
ozes, Martha
ucas, Gregory
urie, Linda
ynch, Elizabeth
ynn, Janet
yon, Curtis
yons, Leola
onon, Daisey
onon, Charles
ominy, Irene
ittle, Uriel
ittle, Nicole
incoln, Connie
ewis, Tameka
ewis, Nolan
ewis, Marjorie
ewis, George
ewis, Fallon
ewis, Darvel
evy, Louis
eslie, Sharon
emoN, John
ehman, Ann
ee, Tonya
ee, Keyonte
ee, Joseph
ee, Carolyn
ee, Brittany
ee, Bernice
edet, Douglas
awrence, Chantel
angs, Randy
angdon, Paul
agarde, Armando
atham, Cassandra Ann
aurent, Elizabeth Savoie
ambert, Armand F.
akiba Joseph, Lakiba
ively, Joel David
andry, Neomi
yons, Carlton
eola, Sam
andry, Merrell
enox, Gilbert
andry, Athelgra
ee, Mayfield
evy, Louis Jr.
ouvier, Geraldine
ucien, Tyrone
ugo, Ivan
Mahaney, Peggy
Major, Frankle
Major, Joseph
Mancuso, Mary
Manuel, Jacqueline
Marcellas, Willia
Mares, Shirley
Marks, George
Marsala, Edna
Marsh, Christina
Marshall, Randall
Marshall, Jr., John
Martin, Maria
Martin, Plummie
Martin, Cecile
Martin, Mary
Martin, Plummie
Martinez, Willie
Martinolich, August
Mascaro, John Lawrence
Masino, Joyce
Mason, Arthur
Matrange, Marjorie
Matthews, Rendy
Mattox, Roger
Maurino, Louise
Maxey, Harneitha
Maxey, Sr., Louis
May, Jessie
Mayfield, Irvin
MayfielD, Lee
Mazerat, Vetina Scorsone
Mc Donald, Matthew
Mc Manus, Wilda
Mccaddy, Paul
Mccarthy, Vera
Mcclanahan, Inez
Mcclendon, Amy C.
Mccray, William
Mcdonald, Matthew
Mcguire, Joyce
Mchugh, Thelma
Mckay, Debbie
Mcmanus, Wilda
Mcneese, Destiny
Mcwilliams, Darrell
Meeks, Patricia
Mejia, Lidia
Melancon, Ethel
Melerine, Lucille

Melvin, Katherine
Meyer, Earl
Meyer, Helen
Meyer, Shirley
Miceli, Lloyd
Michael, Scotty
Migllore, Rose
Milanez, George
Miller, Sydney
MiLler, Willie
Miller, Sr, Arthur
Milton, Darryl
Mogabab, Anees
Mollere, Jane
Monahan, John Joseph
Montalbano, Helen
Moore, Mary
Moore, Shannon
Moore, Victoria
Mora, Edward
Morales, Laureta
Morang, Robert
Morant, Mary
Moreland, Ned
Morris Ii, John James
Morrow, Curtis
Mortellaro, Helen
Mosby, Veola
Mosgrove, Stephen
Moss, Roy
Muhoberac, Matthew
Mullen, Matilda
Mumphrey, Joel
Murphy, Doris
Murphy, Nancy
Muse, Johnathan
Myles, Billy
Mutin, David
Morris, Shirley
MOnroe, Shannon
Modican, Joyce
Mobley, Harry
Mobbs, Annie
Milton, Darryl
Millward, Roderick
Miller, Nemiah
Miller, Nellie
Miller, Kattie
Miles, Dashell
Metzler, Delores
Metz, Charles
Mettlen, Billy
Mesha, Sam
Mervin, Ann
Merriman, Alberta
Mcmillian, Tawain
Mcknight, Harrison
Mckinnis, Vernell
Mcdowel, Curtis
Mcdaniels, Mary
Mccalister, Elsie
Mays, Ralph
Matthews, Florence
Mathieu, Melvina
Mason, Latisha
Marshall, Willie
Marshall, Williams
Marquez, Glenda
MarFo, George
Malbando, Christina
Magee, Edward
Mackey, Ann
Martin, Gladys Livaudais
Mcmillion, George Otto
Mckinley, Dr. Kevin
Martin, Reginald
Mahe, John A.
Mccall, Ishom
Majid, Abdul Kareem
May, Melvin
Mcdonald, Daniel
Mcdonald, Robert Charles
Macconnell, Elizabeth
Myers, Kevin
Mosley, Martin
Macarthur, Lisa
Martinez-Pazmino, Carmen
Morrison, Benson
Mayfield, Lee
Mitchell, Ethel
Martin, Willie
Meunier, Arthur
Miller, Theron Joe
Mitchell, Aaron G.
Morris, Laura
Mortinelli, John
Mckenzie, Sandra
Mattox, Emile William
Melton, G.
Marino, Louise
Marrero, Rosetta
Martin, Judith
Martin, Rovenia
Matthews, Lydia
Mccoy, Alfred
Meyer, Paul
Minor, Willie Mae
Napoleon, William
Navis, Francis
Necaise, Jr., Horace
Neely, Michael Patrick
Nelson, Elaine
Nesossis, Steven
Nettles, Ashley
Nicholas, Joseph
Nora, Edward
Norman, Sr., Lee
Northon, Olga
Norwood, Mary
Nymel, Daryl
Norton, Martin
Norris, Wilbert
Norman, Lee
Nolan, Joseph
Newman, Danny
Nelson, Dennis
Nellius, Valencia
Nellius, Delisa
Naylor, Joseph
Nahar, Waldo

Narcisse, Isiah
Naylor, Joseph
Napoleon, James
Newman, Denise
Olivier, Helen
Olsen, Mary
Orduna, Louis
Owens, David
Owney, Bernadine
Owens, Patricia
Overtree, Ricky
Otero, Judith
Oslem, Stella
Odoms, Leroy
O'hara, John
O'byran, Lark
Olarte, Virginia
Owney, Bernadine
O'conner, Alexis
Oxley, Clifton Eloyce
Owens, David
Deporter, Chyaeka
Paul, Melvin
Pace, Maria
Palfi, Stevenson J.
PaLmer, Thomas
Paolillo, James
Parker, Dorothy
Parker, George
Parker, Janet
Parker, Joe Ben
Parker, Margaret
Parker, Rita
Parker, Rose
Parr, Carol Ann
Parr, Norman
Patterson, Earl
Peel, Dorothy
Pelitere, Peter
Pembo, Marie Louise Bonis
Pereira, Yvette
Perkins, George
Perret, Helen
Perry, Meg
Pesses, Albert Ashley
Peters, Jerry
Peters, Reynette
Peterson, Einer
Peyton, Virginia
Phillips, Beverly
Phillips, Paul
Phillips, Winston
Pichon, Dorothy
Pickett, Glorai Louise Wade
PieRre, Ernest
Pierre, Juanita
Pilet, Irwin Eugene
Pinkney, Thelma
Pino, Rosemary
Pizzuto-Robino, Bernice
Platt, Louise
Poissenot, Emile
Poladura, Helen
Polk, Serena
Polmer, Rachel
Ponseti, Marvin
Porter, William
Prather, Jack
Prather, Jason
Pratt, Ruth
Preston, Larry
Preston, Margaret
Preston, Scott
Preston, Leon
Price, Douglas
Price, Julius
Prima, Joseph
Prusinski, Jerome
Purcell, Christian
Pearsall, Tim David
Pope, Neimiah
Poole, Harold
Pollard, Kebbins
PoLk, Sarena
Platts, Carolann
Pittman-Powers, Lynndia
Piper, Stacey
Pierce, Nancy
Pham, Kim
Perry, Daryl
Perkins, Leroy
Payton, Germisha
Payne, Michael
Paurmelee, Tom
Pauche, Blanche
Patterson, Michael
Patterson, Latoya
Patterson, Kerrione
Patterson, Ernest
Parker, David
Palmore, Mcarther
Porter, Kenneth
Poston, Betty
Poston, Guy
Preston, David
Powell, Andrew
Polmer, Rachel
Payne, Clem
Potterstone, Andrew
Pierce, Christopher
Parker, Willie
Pastrano, Rita
Purchner, Lillian
Pointer, Terry
Peyton, Virginia
Porobil, Bernadine
Puglia, Rosemarie
Patrolia, Gregory
Patrolia, Richard
Patterson, Michael Wayne
Payne, Dorothy
Pierre, Samuel, Jr.
Powers, Hayden
Prieur, Randy
Payton, Joycelyn
Packham-Smith, Toreen
Pierre, Andrea
Patterson, Lawrence
Rainey, Jr., James
Rambo, Glenn Marshall

Ramsey, Kemp
Randall, Gladys
Randolph, Isaac
Ransom, Verina
Rashkin, Janet
Rasmussen, Muriel
Ray, Eddie
Reacord, Althea
Rebstock, Loretta
Reeves, Olampia
Reysack, Jr., Richard George
Richard, Edward
Richard, Sandra
Richards, Milton
Richburg, Lejohn
Rickie, Jeanne
Riehm, Elizabeth Rush
Riehms, Clarise
Riess, Karlem
Risper, Leonard
Rivers, Rufus
Rizzo, Virginia
Roark, Rebecca Ann
Roberts, Dana
Robertson, Arthur
Robertson, Ethel
Robichaux, Edward
Robichaux, Elizabeth
Robichaux, John
Robichaux, Virgie
Robin, Jean
Robinson, Bessie
Robinson, Leroy
Robinson, Pearl
Rocha, Alberto
Rodgers, Zola
Rodrigue, Eva
ROdrigue, Eva
Rodriguez, Jose
Roessler, Guadalupe
Romero, Manuel
Romero, Margarita
Roquevert, Louis
Ross, Elizabeth
Roth, George
Roy, Eddie
Ruddiman, Mary
Ruiz, Ryan Peter
Ruiz, Uk
Ruiz, Uk
Rulh, Ruth
Russell, John
Russell, Robert
Russell, Joshua E.
Ryan, Georgia
Ryan, Van
Ryburn, Alma
Ragusa, Keith
Raiford, Dymania
Randolph, Larenza
Rath, Robert
Ray, Louise
Rayford, Donna
Rayford, Elenora
Raymond, Natasha
Raymond, Orin
Reeves, Norma
Rene, Gretchen
Renouf, Leo
Reynolds, Cary
Rhodes, Kevin
Richards, Farol
Richman, Milton
Ripoll, Anola
Roberson, James
Roberts, Lakeisha
Robertson, Laquish
Robin, Lynda
Robinson, Budnisha
Robinson, Carolyn
Robinson, Keith
Robinson, Percy
Rochon, Roger
Rodriguez, Juniet
Rogers, Louis
Rollins, Katie
Ross, James
Roussell, John
Royl, David
Russell, John
Rendall, Robert
Rankins, Sam
Roach, Ben
Risens, Quintella
Roussell, John
Ridgley, Ryan
Romphf, Donna
Reynolds, Earl
Riley, AMy
Riddick, Terrance
Revia, Denise
Richardson, David
Rhodes, Kevin
Rice, Uk
Richardson, Joseph
Raymond, Felton
Rivera, Efrain
Ruits, Bridgett
Rock, Edgar
Rollins, Willie
Ross, Charlena
Ross, Johnny, Jr.
Silvan, Leonardo
Saia, Darlene
Samuels, Sr., Grady
Sanders, James
Sanders, Lawrence
Sanfilippo, Antonia
Santa Cruz, Michael
Saucier, Odessa
Sauter, Fritz
Savoca, Nicholas
Savoie, Rose
Scariano, Louise
Schielder, Anna
Schiro, Cynthi
Schiro, Delores
Schiro, Jr., Jake
Schmidt, Anna Dahmer
Schneider, Catherine

Schneider, Pat
Schraberg, William
Schultz, Irma
Schultz, John
Scott, Austin
Scott, Bereita
Scott, Joseph
Seabury, John
Seals, Emma
Seals, Joann
Seeger, Elaine
Seifker, Henry
Sennette, Janie
Serou, Gordon
Serpas, Nellie
Sevalia, Barabara
Sevalia, Victoria
Shanks, Isaac
Shannon, Edna
Shaw, Jerry
Shaw, William
Shell, Jr., Charles W.
Shepherd, Walter
Sherman, Lillian
Sherman, Rose
Sherman, Scott
Sherrod, Naomi
SiGnal, Pamela
Simmons, Arthur
Simmons, Jr., Levie
Simon, Richard
Simon, Ruby
Simpson, Mary
Sindibaldi, Albert
Singagliese, Brian
Singelmann, Pauline
Singleton, Bennie
Sires, Louise
Smallwood Jr., Matthew
Smith, Catherine
Smith, Darren
Smith, Elvira
Smith, Freddie
Smith, Janice
Smith, John
Smith, Leon Ray
Smith, Lincoln
Smith, Marsha
Smith, Richard Sherman
Smith, Velzie
Smith/Varnado, Willa
Smooth, Ersell
Smooth, Kendra
Smooth, Kendricka
Snowden, Cynthia
SparkS, Edward
Sparks, Susie
Spears, Jerome
Spichiger, Jean
St Pe, Robert
Stafford, Joseph
Stafford, Mary
Stafford, Mary Ann
Stafford, Sr., Henry
Starks, Edward
Sterns, Marian
Stevens, Eleanor
Stewart, Charles
Stewart, Onita
Stewart, Karl
Stieber, Marian
Stieber, Raymond
Stipelcovich, Betty
Stormant, Anna
Stovall, Cory Chevell
Strong, Nelia
Sullivan, John
Sutton, Edith
Swan, Alvin
Swiber, Madeline
Sylvester, Patricia
Sanders, Mojuan
Sandifer, Eric
Santalucito, Susan
Savoie, Vincent
Scarabin, Wayne
Scott, Author
Scott, Emma
Scott, Leester
Scott, Tamarra
Scott-Jones, Jackie
Selbe, David
Seward, Michael
Shell, Charles
Shelton, Jarrald
Shepard, Geneviede
Shepard, Steze
Silva, Billie
Simmon, Harle
Small, Desy
Small, Theresa
Smiley, Mattie
Smith, Doris
Smith, Edward
Smith, Glen
Smith, Sadie
Smith, Theresa
Smith, Tyrone
Smith, Vernon
Smith, Wayne
Smuk, Teniska
Stephens, Chris
Stephens, Mark
Sterling, Ashley
STevenson, Shontell
Stewart, Christopher
Stewart, Eldridge
Stewart, Lisa
Susberiou, Jasmine
Sauter, Fritz Joseph
St. Pierre, Sr., Albert
Scheets, Mr.
Smith, Kayla
Stewert, Jousha
Stetson, Jean
Smith, Lisa
Shelton Jr., Eddie Lee
Smith, Lydia
Smith, Charles G
Skipper, Cladilia

Smith, Theresa
Stokes, Lakeishama
Scott, Carl
Slayton, Jennifer
Slayton, Robin
Swope, Robert
Scales, Frank
Scott, Micheal
Shimizu, Takashi
Stone, Charles
Steven, Calandria
Smith, Lana
StierlEn-Liuzza, Dominique
Shanil, Gunesekara
Sordelet, Leoma
Shaw, Olympia
Swafford, Jon
Stewart, Louise
Seeler, Elaine
Segnal, Pamela
Singleton, Mary
Sovoca, Nick
Spano, Carole
Sparks, Edward Charles Jr.
Sampson, Clifford
Sanders, William
Tappan, Donald
Tart, John
Tart, Matthew
Tart, Samuel
Tate, Allen
Taylor, James
Taylor, Ronald Lee
Taylor, Jr., Joseph Edward
Thornton, Lillie
Thrift, Carl
Tidwell, Rosalie
Tidwell, Roy
Tobias, Daisy
Toombs, Charles
Torrence, George
Toups, Alice
Toups, Beulah
Trahan, Kim Marie
Tran, Hong
Tran, Nam
Trapolin, Frank
Trentecosta, Mary
Turner, Ebert
Turner, John
Turner, Meaher
Thompson, Terry
Thompson, Minnie
Taquino, Dorothy
Taylor, Charlie
Taylor, Corinne
Taylor, Marilyn
Taylor, Michael
Teepale, Kenny
Thomas, Lee
Thomas, Nichol
Thomas, Shirlean
Thorton, Wayne
Toussaint, Donald
Tran, Phu
Tremel, Carry
Trueblood, Montava
Tyler, Alvin
Tyler, Betty
Tyler, Patricia
Tallon, Arthemise Kelly
Tortorich, CharleS
Tupps, Donald
Tuell, Marcelle
Treemont, Keyuana
Trimmer, Norma
Thompson, Blanche
Tuell, Marcelle
Taylor, Lachristina
Thomas, Joseph
Thomas, Mel
Thomas, Shirlean
Thomas, Shelly Lee
Taylor, Charles
Taylor, Jack
Temple, Tommie
Teno, Joseph
Theodore, Ryan Desmond
Thibodeaux, Emma
Thomas, Earl
Thomas, Meddie
Thomas, Rodney
Thomas, Shelly
Thomason, Michael
Thomopolous, Donna
Thompson, Charles
Uhl, Idamay Hayden
Ulmer, James
Urquhart, Anna
Uyehara, Tony
Valteau, Wendell
Van Schultz, Alan
Varnado, Aden
Varnado, Willa Mae
Vaughn, Pamela
Veal, Mable
Venison, Lee
Verret, Almeda
Vicente, Pedro
Vidrios, Inez
Vierling, Collette M.
Vierling, Gerald
Villars, Margaret Shirley
Vinet, Jr., Steven L.
Valerio, Celesten
Vazquez, Mario
Venable, Alvin
Verret, Michelle
Vincent, Malcou
Vinson, Tina
Virga, George
Vanhowsertanzap, Poaldagota
Vance, Randy Scott
Verette, Leo
Vernandi, Aden
Voigt, Charles W.
Wagner, Mary
Walker, Patricia
Walker, Shirley
WalKer, Willie

Waller, Genevieve
Walls, Rose Marie
Warden, Rita
Warren, James
Washington, Celina
Washington, James
Washington, Rita
Watson, Iretha
Watson, Monroe
Watts, Wilbur
Weathers, James
Weathersby, Mary
Weathersby, Maurice
Weaver, James
Webster, Phyllis
Webster, Thomas
Weems Sr., Charles Edward
Welch, Roland
Wescovich, Henry L.
Wesley, Harrison
White, Arnold
White, Helen
Wickem, Joan
Wilder, James
Wilkins, Mary Elizabeth
Williams, Audrey
Williams, Clarence
WiLliams, David
Williams, George
Williams, Joseph
Williams, Lawrence
Williams, Lionel
Williams, Roy
Williams, Rosetta
Williams, Walter
Williams, Willie
Williams, Yolanda
Williams, Jr., Paul
Wilson, Madge
Wilson, Raymond
Wimberly, Hattie
Woods, Alphonse
Woods, Samuel
Wright, Joseph
Wycoff, William
Walker, Arthur
Walker, Beverly
Walton, Adrian
Warren, Deralica
Warren, Michael
Washington, Dorothy
Washington, Felicia
Washington, Joyce
Washington, Rosylynn
Washington, ShErman
Webb, Eboni
Wells, Charlie
Wesner, Harry
West, Vicky
White, Jaquita
White, Joseph
White, Vernon
Whitlow, Gereld
Whittles, Chanie
Wiggins, Leroy
Williams, Chris
Williams, Claude
Williams, Cleveland
Williams, Evelyn
Williams, Gladius
Williams, Jaye
Williams, Laverne
Williams, Lavience
Williams, Louise
Williams, Margarite
Williams, Rita
Williams, Willie
Wilson, D'artagnan
Wilson, Gerald
Wilson, Lauren
Winchester, William
Windy-Boy, Travis
Womack, Larrine
Worthington, Mark
Wyatt, Matthew
Williams, Lee
Ward Favors, Pansy Elda
Webb, Deborah
Williams, Charles
Wagner, Alma
Washington, Deloris
Williams, Mervin
Waters, Kares
Williams, Melvin
Williams, Maurice
Ward, Reginald
Wilson, Crystal
Wilson, Jean
Woods, Greg
Wilson, Fred, Jr.
Wiemers, Mabel
Womack, Larrine
Wood, Leonard
Walker Sparks, Jacqueline
Wilson, Gail
Woodard, Donald
West, Luther Louis
Williams, Lawrence
Wills, Arthur Joseph Jr.
Wilson, Wilma
West, John
Young, John
YouNg, Gloria
Young, John
Young, Lynus
Young, Robert
Youngblood, Carolyn
Yates, Keyna
Young, Marlon
Young, Roland
Youngblood, Netti
Ybarzabal, Christina
Yancy, Antanisha
Zimmerman, John
Zumpe, Walter
Zeno, Coleman
Zimmerman, Jessica
Ziefle, Robert

CREATED BY TERRENCE SANDERS FOR 'THE SARATOGA COLLECTION' WITH THE SUPPORT OF MARCEL WISZNIA

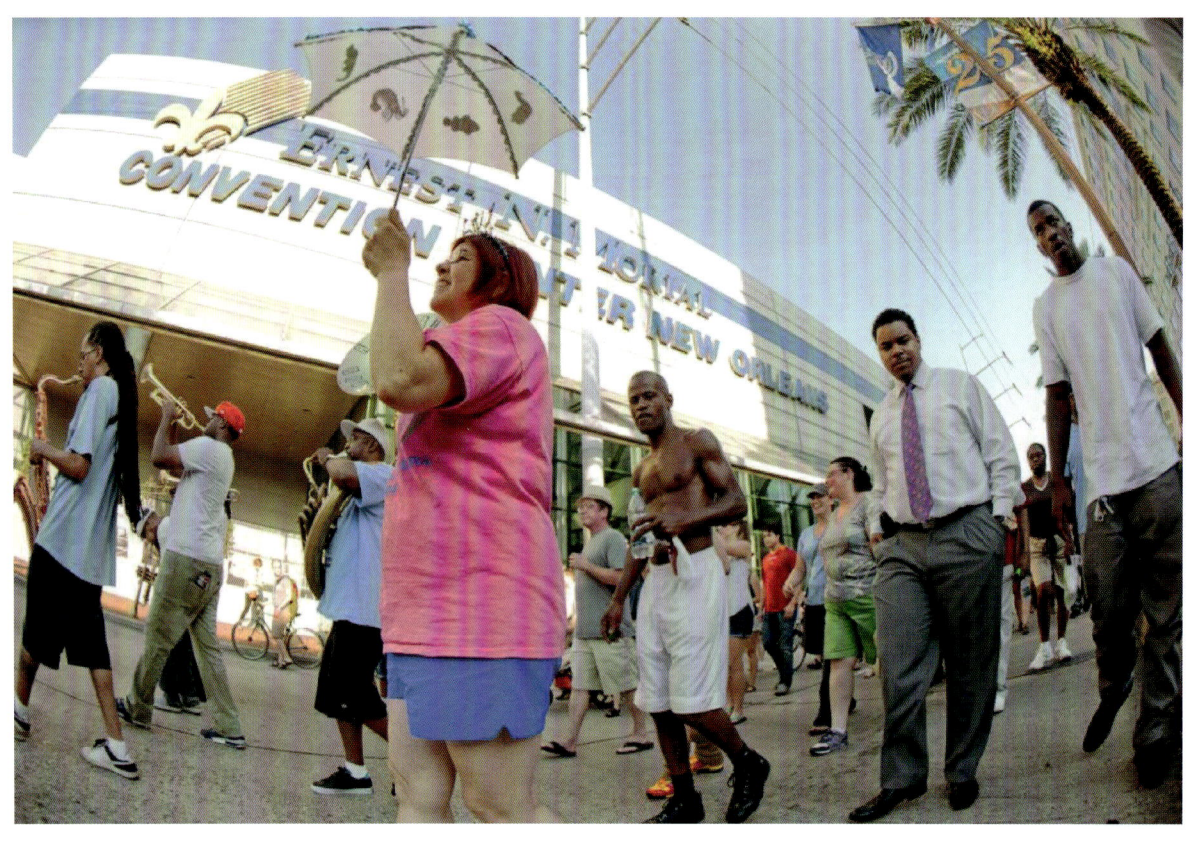

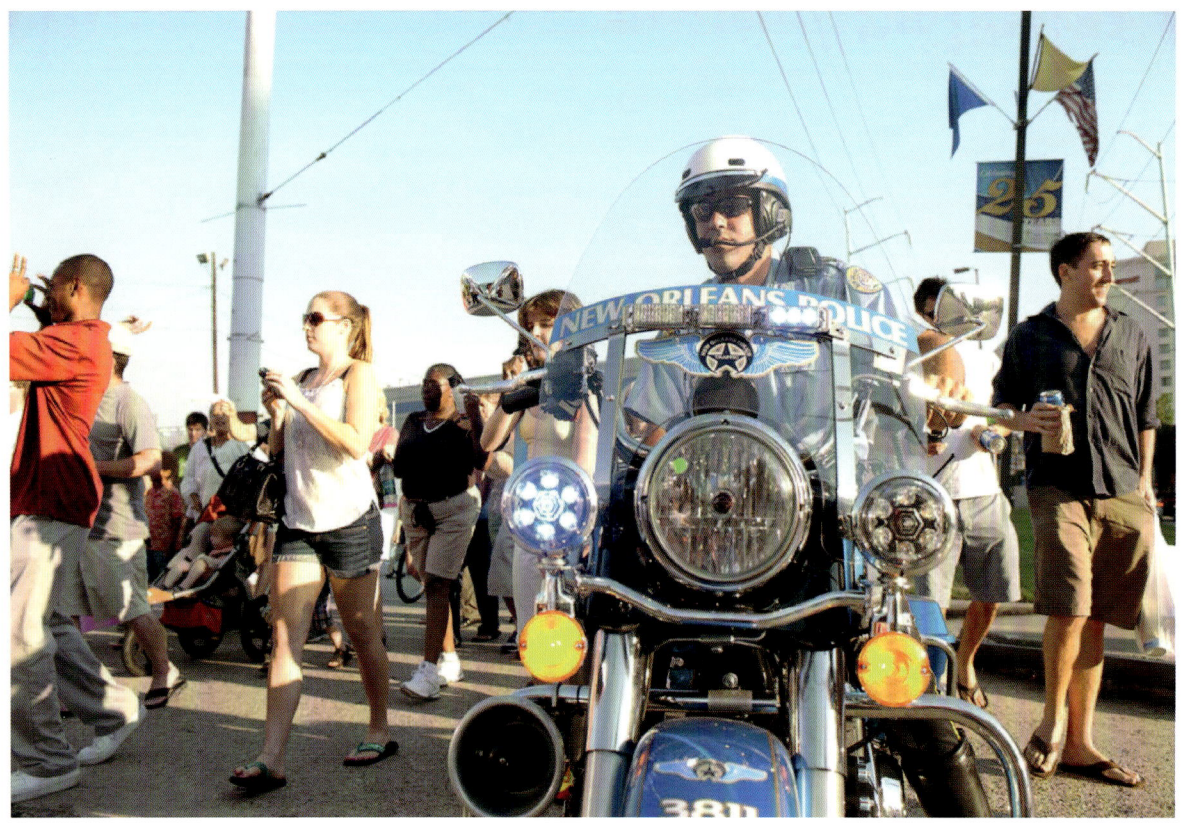

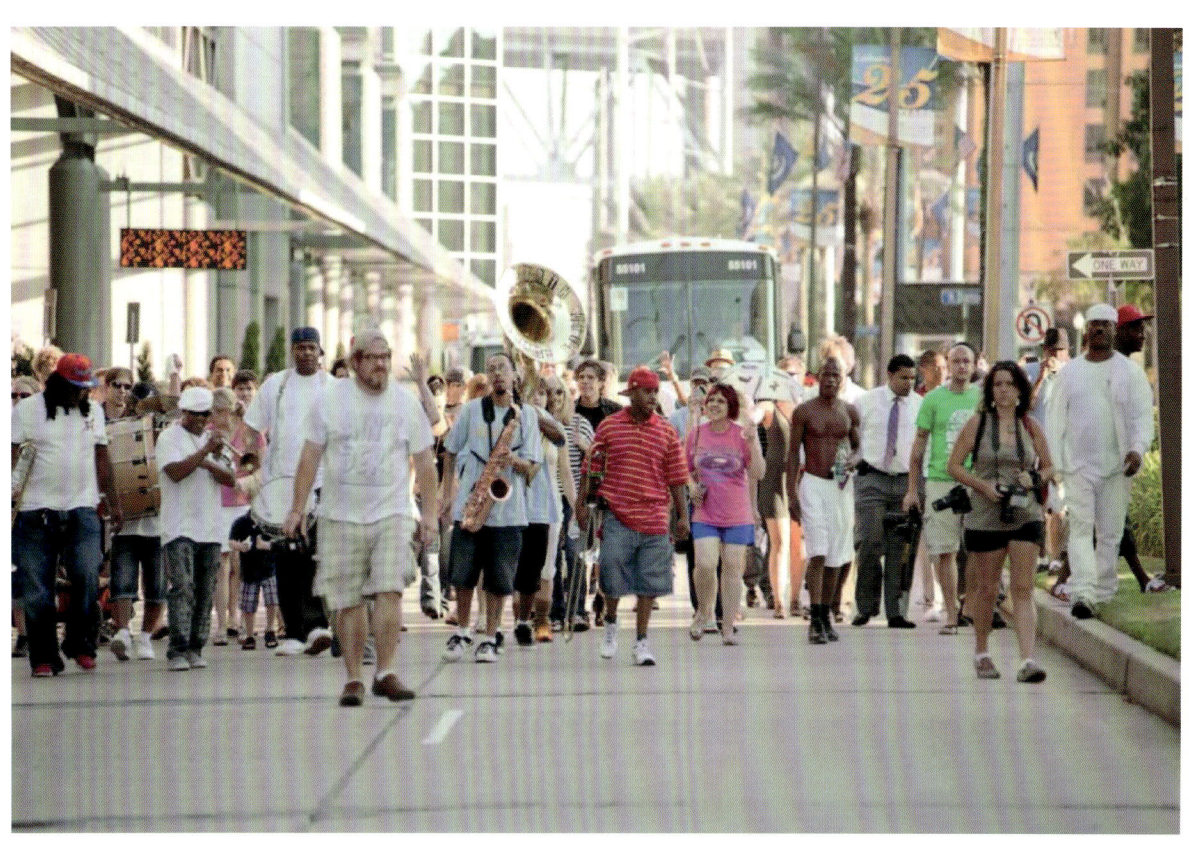

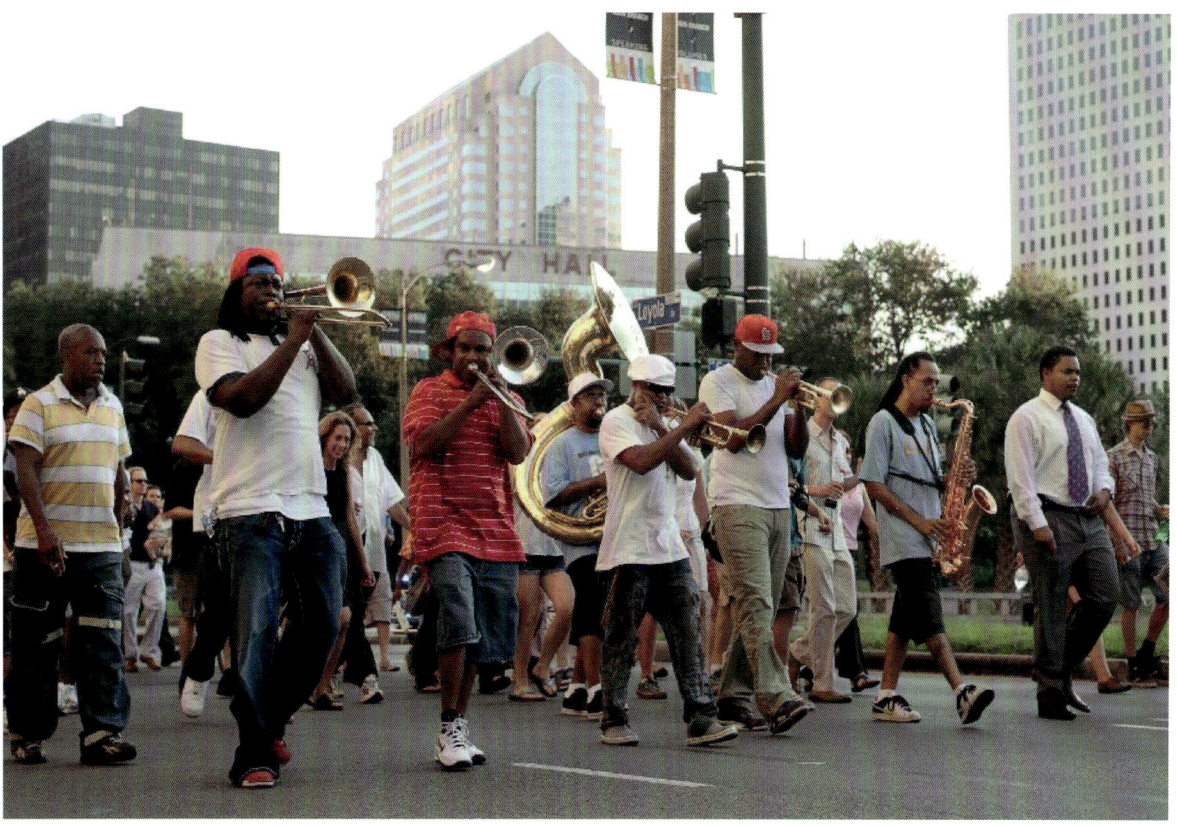

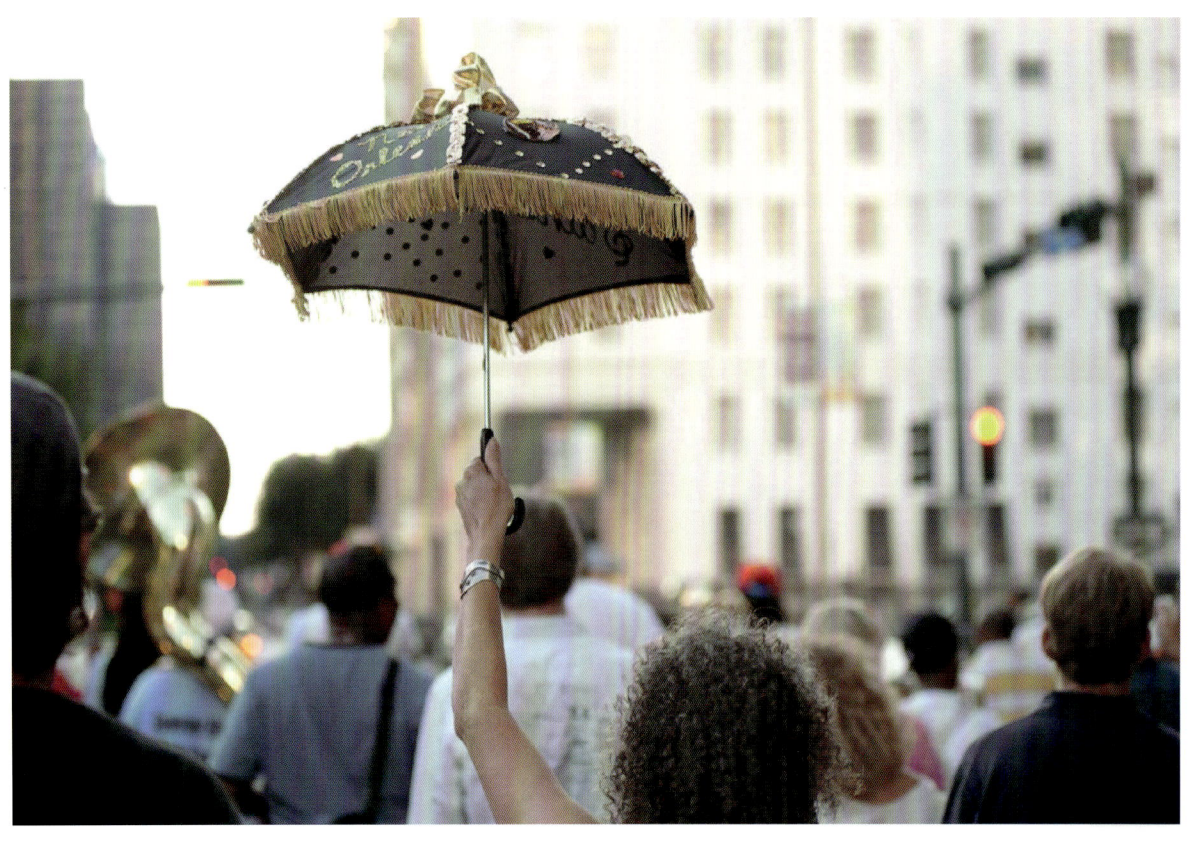

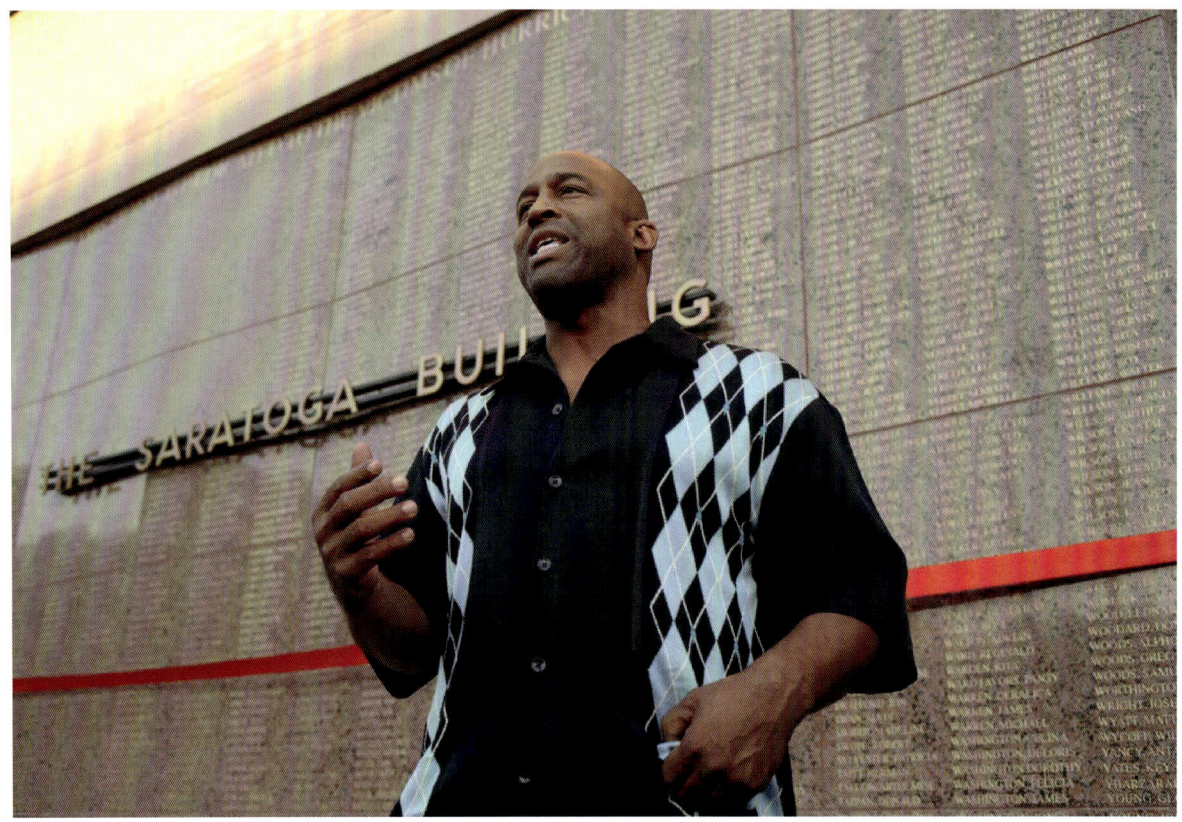

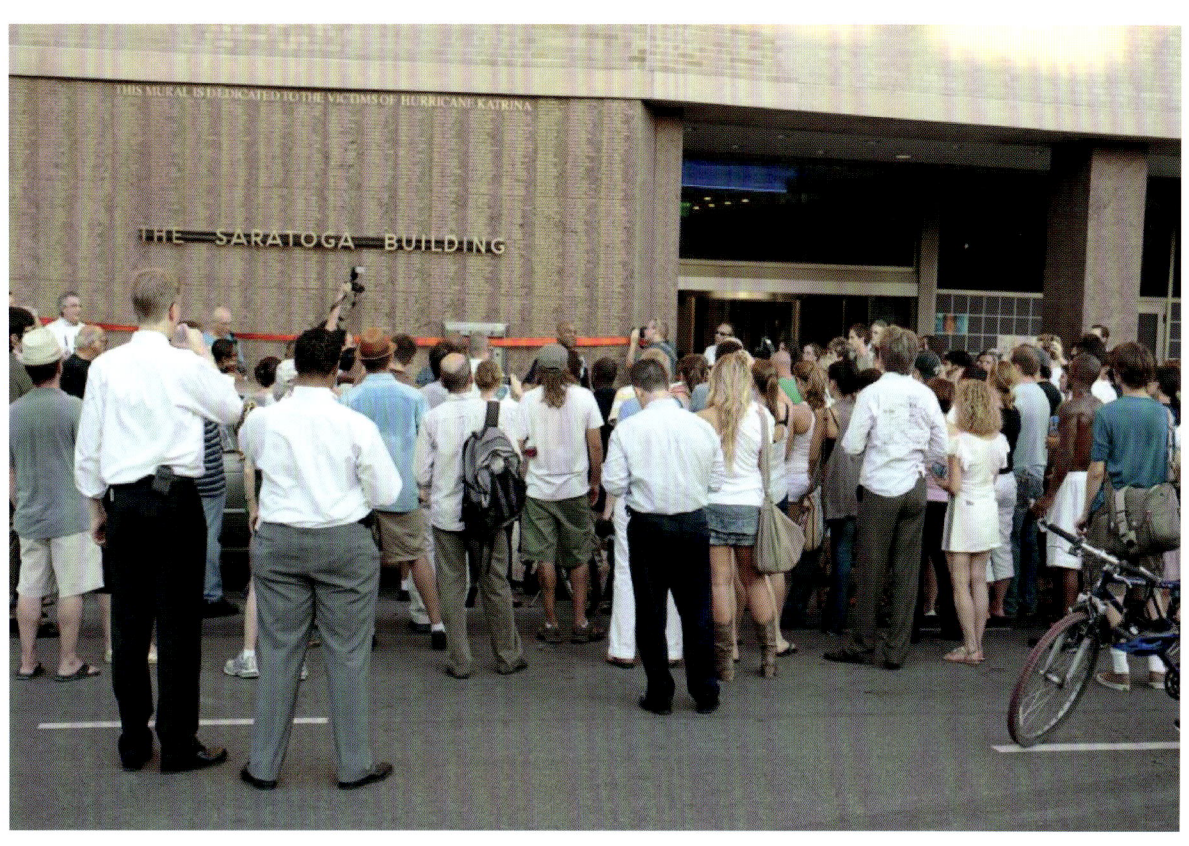

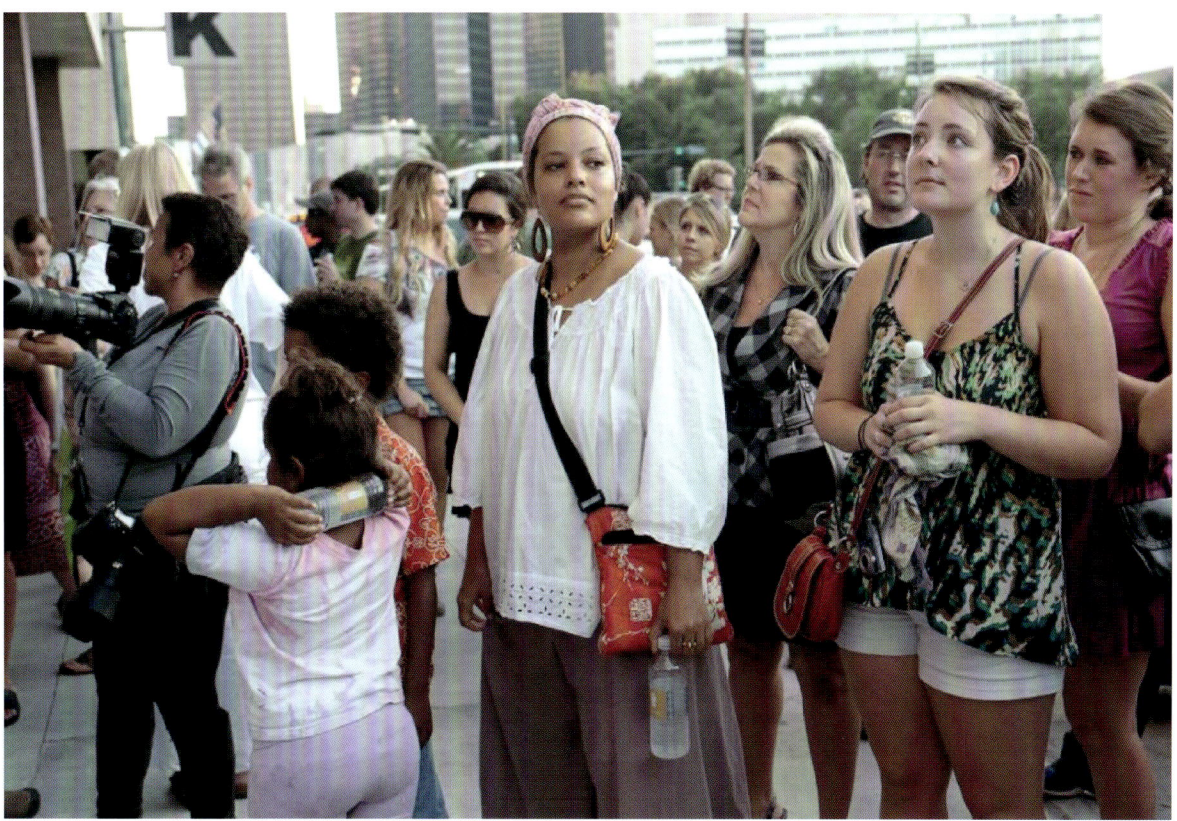

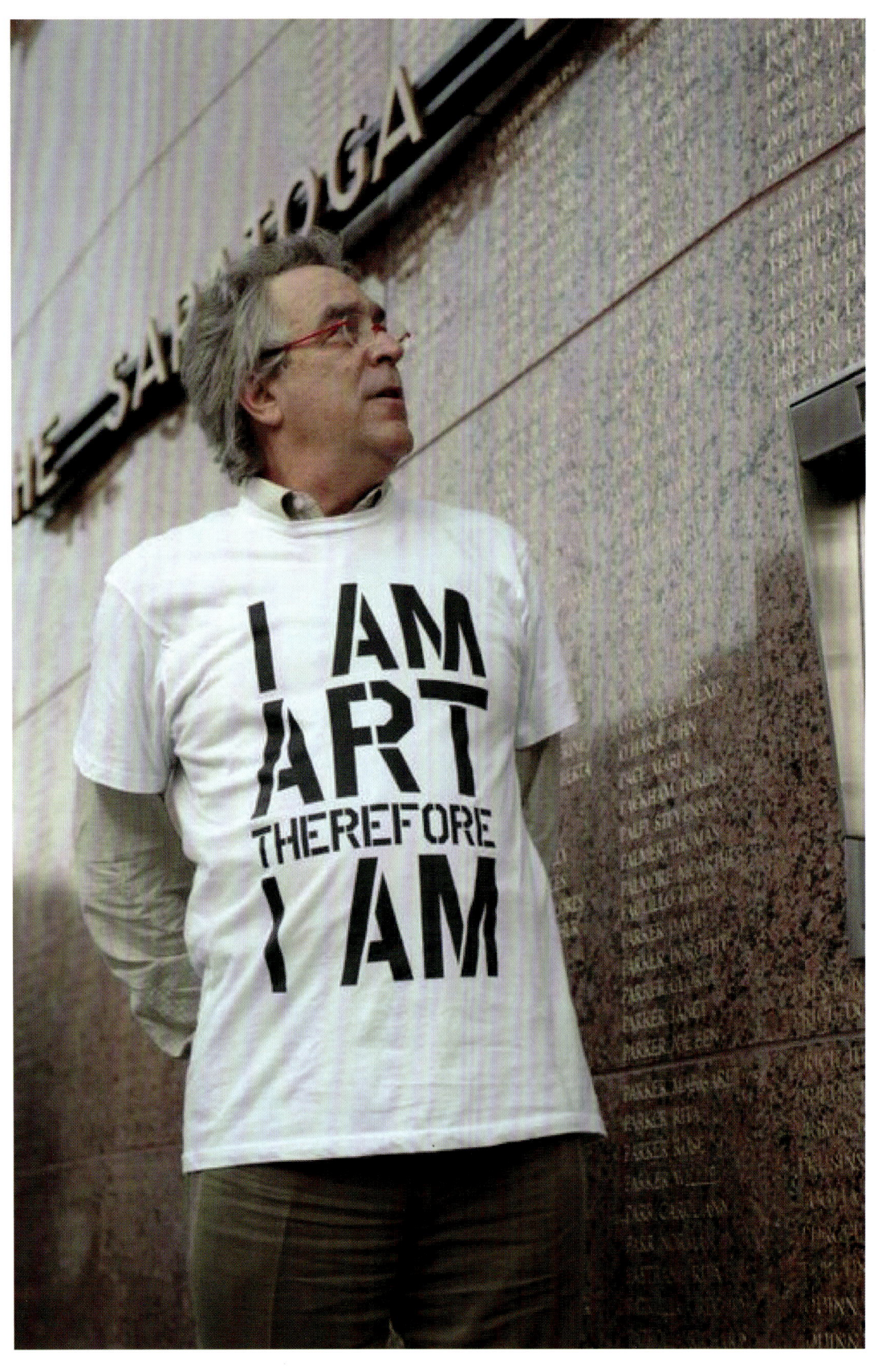